MYTHOLOGICA

written by
Steve Kershaw

illustrated by
Victoria Topping

WIDE EYED EDITIONS

INTRODUCTION

Greek mythology is everywhere. Superstar athletes have the Midas touch, fashion designers have their muses, we undertake Herculean tasks, we make personal odysseys, and we all have our Achilles heel. This book gives you a selection of some of the greatest mortals, immortals, and monsters in Greek mythology.

Human beings are really important in the Greek myths. The stories are full of mighty gods, scary monsters, talking animals, and magic, but the heroes and heroines are amazing mortal men and women with big personalities.

Greek gods and goddesses look like men and women, although they are stronger, more beautiful, and have mysterious powers. Even though they are immortal, they often behave like humans: they are always fighting, arguing, sulking, and doing nasty and unpleasant things. Which makes for great storytelling!

Mythical monsters are awesome and frightening, and even the gods and goddesses can have trouble controlling them. Heroes often have to fight and subdue them so that the world can be a safer place for all of us.

◊ GREEK NAMES ARE HARD

Greek names can be really difficult, and there are lots of different ways of spelling them in English. Achilles is really Akhilleus in Greek; Clytemnestra is actually Klytaimnestra; and Oedipus is called Oidipous. Sometimes the Greek gods and heroes are given Roman names too, so Odysseus becomes Ulysses, and Zeus becomes Jupiter or Jove! So we've chosen the most familiar spellings, but given you their names in real Greek too!

◊ MYTHS ARE IMPORTANT

Greek myths are much more than children's stories...They might, or might not, be true, but this doesn't take away their power. They are traditional tales that are incredibly important to the people who tell them. But they are also free-flowing, adaptable, and very good for us to think about. They help us to understand the world.

CONTENTS

ZEUS

King of the gods. God of the sky, lightning, thunder, law, order, and justice

◆ Zeus was a mature, bearded, powerful man. **He carried all the symbols of a mighty ruler: his thunderbolt and eagle; his scepter and royal robes; and his crown.** A beautiful boy named Ganymede served him nectar and ambrosia, the food of the gods, and Themis, the goddess of law and order, sat beside his throne.

WHERE:
Mount Olympus

Zeus (Ζεύς), "the Father of Gods and Men," was the king of all the gods. His parents were the Titans Cronus and Rheia. Zeus had to use all his might to overthrow his father and beat off challenges to his authority from Gaia. But in the end, he became the permanent ruler of the Universe.

He was the god of the sky and the weather and controlled thunder and lightning. He was the head of all the gods who lived on Mount Olympus. He was also the protector of the household, hospitality, and oaths. He could make people famous or obscure, make weak people strong and strong people humble, and he could crush the proud and make crooked things straight.

Zeus went by many names. He was called the Cloud-Gatherer, Counselor, the Bearer of the Aegis (a magical goatskin cloak decorated with golden tassels, which he used to terrify his enemies), the Avenger of Evil Deeds, the Giver of Favorable Wind, and the Savior. His Will, which he signaled by nodding his head, was the same as the Will of Fate.

> ❝ Zeus is the air, Zeus is the earth, and Zeus is the sky. Zeus is all things, and everything that is more than these. ❞

◆ **The awesome statue of Zeus at Olympia was one of the Seven Wonders of the World.** It was made of gold and ivory, and showed him sitting on his throne, wearing a cloak decorated with animals and lilies, and holding a figure of Nike (goddess of victory), and a staff with his eagle perching on it.

◆ Zeus was married to his sister and long-term partner, Hera. Their children were Hebe, goddess of youth, the war-god Ares, and Eileithyia, goddess of childbirth. But Zeus also had lots of other children with other women—such as the Nine Muses, Artemis and Apollo, Heracles, Helen, and Dionysus. **Which meant that he and Hera were always arguing.**

HERA

Goddess of marriage, women, childbirth, and family

WHERE:
Mount Olympus, but her favorite earthly places were Argos, Sparta, and Mycenae

Hera (Ἥρᾱ) was the queen of the Immortals. Just like her brothers and sisters, she was swallowed by her father, Cronus, the moment she was born. But with the help of the cunning trickster Metis, Zeus managed to fool Cronus into taking a potion that made him vomit up his children.

Hera was the sister and wife of Zeus, who seduced her while he was in the form of a cuckoo. She was the goddess of marriage, women, family, and childbirth, as well as the sky and the stars. She was unbelievably beautiful, and all of the Olympian gods and goddesses respected and honored her.

Hera hated and was extremely jealous of Zeus's many lovers and illegitimate children, especially Heracles. She also hated any mortals who dared cross her. The only thing in the whole Universe that Zeus really feared was her temper tantrums, and he was never able to stop Hera tormenting his lovers and his offspring. Hera watched Zeus constantly when he went down to Earth—she could never be fooled, and always knew what he was up to.

She supported the Greeks in the Trojan War, because Paris chose Aphrodite instead of her as the most beautiful goddess.

> **66** The only thing in the whole Universe that Zeus really feared was her temper tantrums. **99**

◊ Hera was a beautiful woman, who had **dignity and a royal air about her**. She was described as "cow-eyed" or "cow-faced," and "white-armed." She was often found sitting on a throne, wearing a crown, and holding a scepter tipped with a lotus flower and a pomegranate, to represent fertility.

◊ Zeus and Hera used to fight all the time. When she sent some terrible storms after Heracles, Zeus was so angry that he **tied anvils to her feet and an unbreakable band of gold around her wrists**. He then hung her by her wrists from Mount Olympus.

◊ Hera is often accompanied by a cow, lion, cuckoo, hawk, or peacock. **Her chariot was pulled by peacocks, whose tails were adorned with the eyes of the Giant Argus Panoptes**. Peacocks represented immortality because the Greeks believed their bodies didn't decay after death.

THE TWELVE LABORS OF HERACLES

Heracles was the mightiest of all the Greek heroes. He was the son of Zeus and Alcmene—who was not Zeus's wife. Because of this, Zeus's wife, Hera, absolutely hated Heracles. In a fit of madness, Hera convinced Heracles to kill his own family.

After recovering from his madness, Heracles deeply regretted his actions. He was told to do ten Labors to make up for it, and his uncle Eurystheus of Mycenae chose what the Labors would be.

1 ◊ The first Labor was to bring his uncle the **skin of the terrifying Nemean lion**. Heracles's arrows bounced off its impenetrable golden fur, so he chased it down and, using his amazing strength, captured it with his bare hands.

2 ◊ The next Labor was to kill the **Hydra of Lerna, a monstrous water-snake with multiple heads**. As soon as Heracles destroyed one head, two more grew up in its place. Heracles's nephew Iolaus helped Heracles by using fire to singe the monster's neck after Heracles had chopped the heads off. This stopped new ones sprouting, but Eurystheus said this Labor didn't count, because Heracles hadn't done it on his own.

3 ◊ Labor number three was to capture the **golden-horned Ceryneian hind alive**. Heracles tracked it for a whole year, and eventually he wounded the exhausted animal, slung it on his shoulders, and headed for Mycenae to show it to his uncle.

4 ◊ For his next Labor, Heracles had to bring back the **savage Erymanthian boar**. He shouted and roared, driving the beast out of its lair, chased it into the deep snow, and caught it.

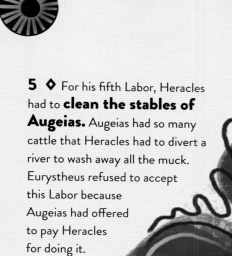

5 ◇ For his fifth Labor, Heracles had to **clean the stables of Augeias.** Augeias had so many cattle that Heracles had to divert a river to wash away all the muck. Eurystheus refused to accept this Labor because Augeias had offered to pay Heracles for doing it.

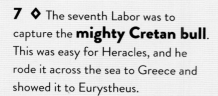

6 ◇ Next, Heracles had to chase away the **huge man-eating, bronze-beaked, Stymphalian birds**, which shot their feathers like arrows. Heracles drove them from the trees by shaking a bronze rattle. They took flight, and Heracles shot them down with his arrows.

7 ◇ The seventh Labor was to capture the **mighty Cretan bull**. This was easy for Heracles, and he rode it across the sea to Greece and showed it to Eurystheus.

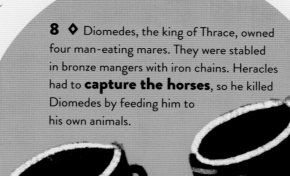

8 ◇ Diomedes, the king of Thrace, owned four man-eating mares. They were stabled in bronze mangers with iron chains. Heracles had to **capture the horses**, so he killed Diomedes by feeding him to his own animals.

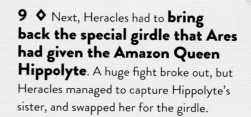

9 ◇ Next, Heracles had to **bring back the special girdle that Ares had given the Amazon Queen Hippolyte**. A huge fight broke out, but Heracles managed to capture Hippolyte's sister, and swapped her for the girdle.

10 ◇ For his tenth Labor, Heracles had to **steal the red cattle belonging to the three-bodied monster Geryon**. He killed Geryon's herdsman and his two-headed guard dog Orthos, and then took care of Geryon with one of his venom-soaked arrows. He sailed home to Greece with the cattle in the golden bowl of the sun god. But Eurystheus insisted on two more Labors...

11 ◇ First Heracles had to **steal the Golden Apples from the Hesperides** (the "Daughters of Evening"), who lived in a garden beyond the sunset, where Atlas held up the sky. A serpent with a hundred heads, helped the Hesperides to watch over the apple tree. Heracles shot the serpent with his poisoned arrows, and then got Atlas to fetch the apples for him, while he held up the Heavens.

12 ◇ Finally, **Heracles had to bring back Cerberus, the multi-headed guard dog of the Underworld**, without using weapons. He used his mighty muscles to haul the beast up to the world of the living. Eurystheus was satisfied, and Cerberus was sent back to where he belonged.

The Labors were complete, and Heracles was taken up to Mount Olympus, where he achieved immortality because of his incredible achievements.

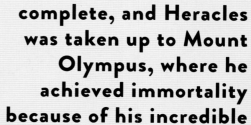

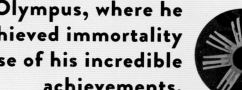

◇ Athena was armed with a shield and spear, and a crested helmet with a sphinx and griffins carved on it. **She was terrifying in battle**—lightning flashed from her armor, fearful snakes breathed fire from her invincible shield, the crest of her great helmet brushed the clouds, and Mount Olympus shook.

◇ Athena was a strikingly beautiful woman with remarkable eyes. She was often called "Glaucopis," which means **"gray-eyed"** (in a gleaming silvery sort of way), **"bright-eyed,"** or **"owl-faced"** (because her eyes were like those of an owl). She often carried an owl, which became the emblem of the Athenians, and was a symbol of wisdom.

ATHENA

Goddess of wisdom, handicraft, and warfare

WHERE:
Athens

Athena (Ἀθηνᾶ) was the daughter of Zeus and Metis. Zeus was warned that after Athena was born, Metis would have a son who would take over from Zeus as king of Heaven. Because of this, Zeus swallowed the pregnant Metis. When the time for the birth had come, Zeus's son Hephaestus split Zeus's head open with an ax, and Athena leaped out, fully armed.

She was the very intelligent virgin goddess of wisdom and domestic arts, and also the goddess of war. She was totally awesome in battle and used intelligent fighting, rather than brute strength, to defeat her enemies. After an amazing competition with her uncle Poseidon, Athena became the special goddess of the city of Athens. Poseidon smashed his trident into the ground and a saltwater spring started to flow; Athena planted the first ever olive tree, which the Athenians thought was a more useful gift. Because of this, she took control of the land and named the city Athens after herself. The olive branch became one of her sacred symbols.

> " She was totally awesome in battle and used intelligent fighting, rather than brute strength, to defeat her enemies. "

◇ Athena wore an ankle-length robe that was adorned with the aegis. This amazed even the gods. **It was a snake-fringed cape that crashed like lightning**, and had the ghastly, fearful head of the Gorgon Medusa in the center, and strong serpents breathing blasts of fire.

APOLLO

◇ Apollo was an awesome musician. He would put on his divine, perfumed musician's robe and enchant the gods by playing his stringed instrument using a golden plectrum. **His music was so magical that he built the walls of Troy just by playing his lyre.**

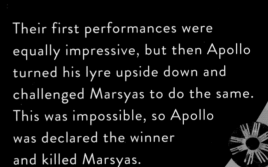

God of music, poetry, art, oracles, archery, plague, medicine, sun, light, and knowledge

WHERE:

His birthplace of Delos and his shrine at Delphi

Apollo (Ἀπόλλων) **was the son of Zeus and a Titan, Leto. He was born under a palm tree on the island of Delos along with his twin sister, Artemis.**

Apollo helped mortals and protected them from evil. He was the god of

many things: prophecy and oracles; light and enlightenment; healing, plague, and disease; purification; music, song, and poetry; archery; and the sun. He was also known as Phoebus ("Shining" or "Brilliant"), and sometimes appeared with a halo—although he would also wear a crown or a wreath and sometimes carry a laurel branch.

It was dangerous to compete with him. The Satyr Marsyas was an incredible flute player and challenged Apollo to a contest. The winner could do whatever he liked to the loser.

Their first performances were equally impressive, but then Apollo turned his lyre upside down and challenged Marsyas to do the same. This was impossible, so Apollo was declared the winner and killed Marsyas.

◇ **Apollo was a beautiful, beardless young man with long hair and delicate good looks.** Rays of light rose from his forehead, his eyes shone with divine brightness, but his smile was always mixed with anger.

◇ **The Greeks thought that the Temple of Apollo at Delphi stood at the "belly button of the world."** It was home to Apollo's priestess, the Pythia, who gave strange prophecies and good advice. Her motto was "Nothing in Excess."

◇ **Artemis has close links with the moon, magic, and wild animals.** Her sacred animal was the deer, and she often drove a chariot pulled by them. The golden-horned Ceryneian Hind was an enormous deer that was also special to her—Heracles had to catch it as one of his Twelve Labors.

◇ Artemis carried a bow and arrow and had all kinds of other hunting equipment—a quiver, spears, torches, and a pack of dogs. **Hunters would sing hymns to her as they set out on their expeditions,** and pray that their nets and snares would be full of prey.

◇ **She liked to wear a crown or a tiara,** which was sometimes decorated with a crescent moon. When she was out hunting, she would wear a short tunic and high boots, perhaps with the pelt of a deer across her shoulders.

ARTEMIS

Goddess of the hunt, forests, hills, the moon, and archery

WHERE:
In the great outdoors

Artemis (Ἄρτεμις) **was the twin sister of Apollo. She was the Greek goddess of hunting and wild animals, but also looked after young girls until they got married, and although she was a virgin herself, she also took care of women in childbirth.**

Artemis was a very tall, fit, athletic, healthy young woman. Yet she could also be wild and very dangerous. Forgetting to sacrifice to her could result in terrible punishments, and it was never a good idea to challenge or offend her.

The hunter Actaeon was tragically eaten by his own dogs because he accidentally saw Artemis while she was bathing naked on Mount Cithaeron. Artemis was so embarrassed and furious that she transformed Actaeon into a stag. His hunting dogs caught his scent, chased after him, and devoured him without realizing who he was.

When the mortal woman Niobe boasted that having fourteen children made her better than Artemis's mother, Leto, who only had two, Artemis killed all of Niobe's daughters. Niobe was transformed into a rock from which tears flowed night and day.

Artemis also hated the fact that her hunting companion Callisto was seduced by Zeus. When Artemis found out that the girl was pregnant, she changed her into a bear. Zeus later transformed Callisto into the constellation of the Great Bear.

POSEIDON

God of the sea, earthquakes, soil, storms, and horses

WHERE:

His palace is in the sea, near Aegae on the island of Euboea

Zeus's brother Poseidon (Ποσειδῶν) was an imposing, well-built, mature god, who had a very fine beard. He was the lord of the sea and earthquakes and was called "the god who circles the Earth and shakes it." He also had a close connection with horses and bulls.

Poseidon helped to build the walls of Troy, and in the battle between the gods and the Giants, he chased the Giant Polybotes through the sea, broke a piece off the island

of Cos, and threw it on top of him.

He was also the father of some Giants, including Antaeus, who used to kill strangers by making them wrestle with him, and then decorated his father's temple with their skulls. Poseidon's son Orion was a mighty hunter who could either walk on the surface of the sea, or wade through it because he was so tall. His wife was ox-eyed Amphitrite, although she wasn't the mother of his children Polyphemus the Cyclops, the winged horse Pegasus, or the hero Theseus. Poseidon granted Theseus three curses, which he accidentally used to kill his own son Hippolytus, who died in a chariot crash when a terrifying bull appeared from the sea and made his horses stampede.

◊ **At the Isthmian Games, which were held in Poseidon's honor**, the winning athletes were all given crowns made out of wild celery. It was one of Poseidon's sacred plants and he often wore a wreath made out of it.

◊ You can always recognize Poseidon by his trident—a three-pronged fisherman's spear. **He used this to cause earthquakes, destroy his enemies, make springs of saltwater appear, or just to go fishing.** Sometimes he brandished a huge rock encrusted with fish, octopi, and other sea creatures.

◊ **Poseidon rode in a chariot pulled by hippocamps** (sea creatures with the head of a horse, green scales, and snakelike fishy tails), or horses with bronze hooves and golden manes. The sea became calm when his chariot approached. Sea monsters would recognize it and play around him.

◇ Doves, the birds of love, pulled Aphrodite's chariot; the hare was her animal because it was always having babies; the pomegranate was her fruit because of its rich seeds; **and the rose was her flower, stained red when she cut her feet on its thorns** as she tried to help her dying lover Adonis.

◇ **When the three beautiful goddesses Hera, Athena, and Aphrodite quarreled over a golden apple** bearing the words "for the fairest," the Trojan prince Paris decided that Aphrodite should have it. This started the Trojan War.

APHRODITE

Goddess of love and beauty

WHERE:
Cyprus

Aphrodite (Ἀφροδίτη) **was the goddess of love. She grew in the foam of the sea, which the Greeks called aphros, which is where her name comes from. She was often accompanied by her son Eros, and together they were an irresistible force of nature, putting love and passion into the hearts of animals so that they would reproduce.**

Aphrodite was the most beautiful woman in the Universe, and spread love among the gods, men, and women. She often walked around naked, but when she dressed up, she would clean her lovely features with fragrant balms and wear sweet-smelling clothes that were rich and brightly colored with lots of jewelry. Her stunning dress was made by the Graces and Seasons. It was dyed with spring flowers and shone with the brightness of fire. It was enriched with marvelous needlework that shimmered like the moon, and she added lovely necklaces, gorgeous brooches, and shining earrings in the form of flowers.

◇ **Aphrodite's magical girdle was woven with the irresistible powers of love and desire**. It was elaborate and beautifully patterned, with pictures of passion, love, and the whispered terms of endearment that steal the heart away, even from thoughtful people.

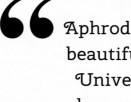 Aphrodite was the most beautiful woman in the Universe, and spread love among the gods, men, and women. "

HEPHAESTUS

God of fire, metalworking, stonemasonry, forges, the art of sculpture, and blacksmiths

◇ Hephaestus was disabled. **His feet were back to front, so he had to walk with the aid of a stick.** Sometimes, though, he rode on a donkey, or used a special wheeled chair or chariot to get around. He also created some intelligent, talking golden attendants who looked like living young women, who assisted his mobility.

◇ **He made some of the most incredible things in the world**: the palaces, thrones, weapons, and chariots of the gods; Zeus's thunderbolts; armor for heroes like Achilles, Heracles, and King Memnon of the Ethiopians; amazing temples and statues; palaces for mortal kings; gold and silver watchdogs; bronze bulls; exquisite jewelry; and Pandora, the first woman.

◇ Hephaestus was assisted by the one-eyed, metalworking Cyclopes. **He created his wonders using his anvil, a mighty hammer and tongs, and a huge set of bellows**. He used a sponge to wipe his brow, and to clean his hands, neck, and chest. He kept his precious tools in a silver strongbox.

WHERE:
On Mount Olympus or under Mount Etna

Hephaestus (Ἥφαιστος) was the god of fire, blacksmiths, craftsmen, metalworking, stonemasonry, carpentry, sculpture, and volcanoes—the Romans called him Vulcan. You could often find him sweating over his bellows and anvil, making something amazing.

Hephaestus was thought to be a rather ugly god. He married Aphrodite, the goddess of love, although their marriage didn't last. Hephaestus was proud of his powerful physique—his massive neck, his hairy chest, and the great big muscles of his arms, and although he walked with a limp, his shrunken legs moved lightly and nimbly beneath him.

He was also good in a fight, and in the Battle of the Gods and Giants, he killed Mimas using missiles of red-hot iron. And he certainly wasn't stupid. When Aphrodite was cheating on him with her lover Ares, he cunningly caught them in the act, and trapped them under an unbreakable net, to the great delight of the gods. Hephaestus also helped with the birth of Athena, using his ax to split Zeus's head open so that the goddess could emerge into the world.

HERMES

Messenger of the gods, god of trade, thieves, travelers, sport, athletes, border crossings, and the guide to the Underworld

WHERE:
Moving easily between the Underworld and the world of the living

Hermes (Ἑρμῆς) was the son of Zeus and Maia, a shy nymph with beautiful hair. Hermes was full of tricks, and the Romans called him Mercury.

Hermes grew up amazingly fast—he was born at dawn, and by the same afternoon, he could play beautiful music on the lyre, which he made out of a tortoise shell.

That same evening, Hermes stole Apollo's cattle. Apollo offered a reward for any information that might lead to the animals' recapture. The Satyrs, a group of human male creatures with horses' ears and tails, agreed to join the search.

Hermes didn't want to be found, so to mislead his followers, he reversed the hooves of the cattle, so that their front hooves faced backward and their back ones faced forward. The Satyrs were confused by the tracks leading in various directions...but the strange sounds of Hermes's music soon gave him away. Apollo quickly caught up with Hermes but became so entranced with the lyre that he swapped the cattle for it.

> ❝ Hermes grew up amazingly fast—he was born at dawn, and by the same afternoon, he could play beautiful music on the lyre. ❞

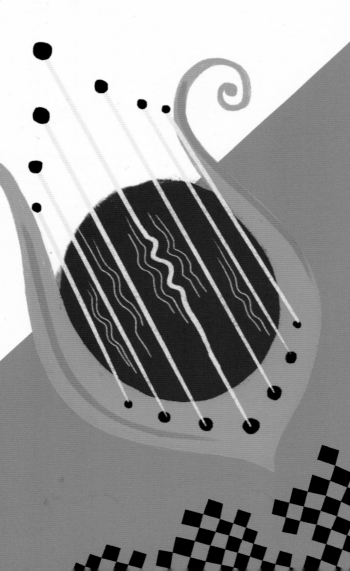

◇ **You can recognize Hermes by his clothes and accessories.** He carries a messenger bag, wears winged boots or sandals, and often makes his journeys wearing a broad-brimmed traveler's hat or a winged cap. He sometimes carried a short sword to protect himself.

◇ **After Hermes invented the lyre, he also made himself some panpipes (the syrinx).** Apollo loved the panpipes so much that in exchange for them he gave Hermes the caduceus—a marvelous wand of blessing and fortune, in the form of a winged staff with two snakes entwined around it.

◇ **Hermes moved swiftly on land and in the air and was very graceful and athletic.** His sacred animals included the ram (sometimes he would ride on the back of one) and the hare, but he was also linked to cattle, sheep, and goats. Hermes's sacred plants were the crocus flower and the strawberry tree.

DIONYSUS

◊ **Dionysus brought extreme happiness and terrible sadness**, but he was always smiling, even when he was doing weird and terrible things, like turning pirates into dolphins!

The god of wine, theater, and the state of ecstasy

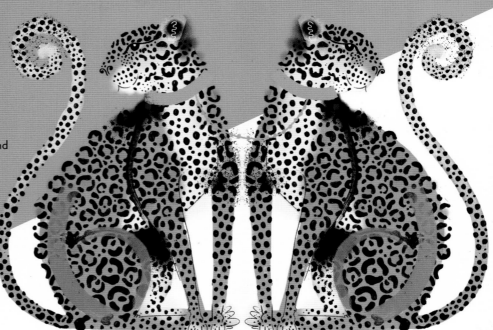

◊ **Panthers were sacred to Dionysus**, and he could often be found riding on their backs, or driving a chariot pulled by a pair of them.

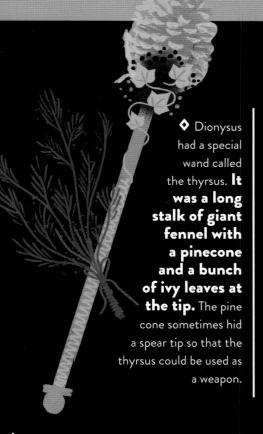

◊ Dionysus had a special wand called the thyrsus. **It was a long stalk of giant fennel with a pinecone and a bunch of ivy leaves at the tip.** The pine cone sometimes hid a spear tip so that the thyrsus could be used as a weapon.

◊ **Dionysus loved exotic clothes.** Although he was a Greek god, he liked to wear rich, colorful, Persian-style robes, or fawn skins. He also loved the theater and would wear actors' costumes. The Greeks put on plays to honor him. The actors always wore masks when they performed, and Dionysus even appeared onstage himself, as a character in terrifying tragedies and hilarious comedies.

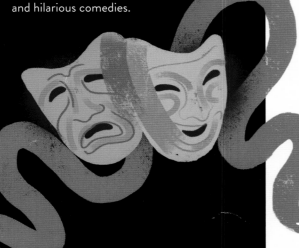

WHERE:
In the mountains of Greece, where the earth flows with milk, wine, and honey

Dionysus (Διόνυσος), also known as Bacchus, was born twice. When Zeus's lover Semele became pregnant with Dionysus, his jealous wife, Hera, tricked Semele into asking Zeus to appear to her in his full divine majesty. This involved thunderbolts and lightning, and Semele was burned to a crisp. But Zeus rescued the child from her body, sewed him up in his thigh, and when the time was right, Dionysus was born again.

He grew up to be a strange and powerful god. He loved wine, the theater, and being out of control. He had some crazy companions called Satyrs, who were part-horse, part-man, and who loved music, chasing girls, and partying. His female followers were "mad women" called Maenads or Bacchae. When Dionysus took control of them, they went wild with wine, music, song, and dance, entering a passionate trance-like state called ecstasy. They dressed in fawn skins with ivy wreaths, and sometimes wore snakes as belts. The Maenads worshipped Dionysus by dancing on the mountains, waving the thyrsus and brandishing torches. Their wild rituals sometimes ended with them tearing animals apart and eating raw meat.

It was always dangerous to resist Dionysus, and you never really knew where you stood with him.

HADES

"Hades drew the lot of mists and darkness and became the king of the Underworld."

God of the dead and the Underworld

WHERE:
The Underworld

Hades (Ἅδης) was the overlord of the Underworld—the god of the dead. The Greeks also called him Pluton ("the Giver of Wealth"), and the Romans knew him as Dis.

Hades was the son of the two Titans, Cronus and Rhea. His brothers were Zeus and Poseidon. Because of a prophecy that told Cronus he would be dethroned by his own son, Cronus swallowed Hades at birth, along with several of his siblings. However, Zeus made Cronus spit his children back up, and together they defeated the Titans in a violent battle called the Titanomachy and imprisoned them down in the pit of Tartarus.

Zeus, Poseidon, and Hades then drew lots to determine what part of the world they would rule. Zeus got the wide sky, Poseidon got the gray sea, and Hades drew the lot of mists and darkness, and became the king of the Underworld. Hades took care of funerals and made sure that dead people got a proper burial.

He also looked after the resources of the earth, such as the fertile soil and precious metals.

◇ Hades is the name of the god, but it is also the name of his kingdom—the Underworld itself. **It was a gray, depressing, silent place, full of ghosts and monsters.** The dead souls had to pay the grim ferryman with a coin to get across the River Styx to their proper resting place.

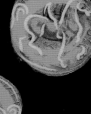

◇ Hades's sacred animal was the screech owl, and his sacred plants included asphodel, mint, and white poplar. **He was often accompanied by the Furies and the Hell-hound Cerberus**, as well as his wife, Persephone, the queen of the Underworld, who he abducted from Earth after falling in love with her

◇ **Hades was a big, intimidating, kingly-looking man with a full, bushy beard.** He carried a scepter with a bird on it, or a horn of plenty, and sat on an ebony throne. His golden chariot was pulled by four immortal black horses, and he wore a helmet that could make him invisible.

◆ Demeter was a mature woman with slender feet and beautiful golden hair. They called her "Demeter of the Lovely Tresses," "Rich-Haired Demeter," and "Reverend Goddess." She would often wear a crown and hold a torch, **as well as sheaves of wheat or a cornucopia (horn of plenty) to show how fruitful she was**.

◆ **When Demeter was mourning the loss of her daughter**, she would tear the covering on her gorgeous divine hair with her hands, throw her dark cloak down from both her shoulders, and wander all over the Earth with flaming torches in her hands.

◆ Even though Demeter was often miserable, **she still had an amazing divine radiance**. Beauty spread all around her, a lovely perfume came from her sweet-smelling robes, and a light shone from her body and golden hair that had the brightness of lightning.

DEMETER
AND PERSEPHONE

Demeter: Goddess of agriculture, harvest, fertility, and sacred law

Persephone: Goddess of the underworld, springtime, flowers, and vegetation

WHERE:
In the fertile fields of Greece

Demeter (Δημήτηρ) **was the goddess of corn and fertility of the land. She had a daughter named Persephone, who the Greeks also called Kore, meaning "the Girl."**

Persephone became the queen of the Underworld when her uncle Hades fell in love with her at first sight. Hades hatched a wicked plan to steal Persephone away.

When Persephone was in a meadow in Sicily one day, she bent down to pick a bunch of flowers.

The moment she did this, the earth opened up and Hades burst out in his golden four-horse chariot. He grabbed the terrified girl and took her down to the Underworld. Demeter fell into a wild panic and set off in search of her kidnapped daughter.

Demeter was the corn goddess and withheld her fruits from the world because of Hades's crime. This caused a terrible famine, and Zeus knew he had to do something. He ordered Hades to give Persephone back. He agreed but not before he gave Persephone some pomegranate seeds to eat. It was a trick. Because she had eaten Underworld food, Persephone now had to stay with Hades for half of every year. For that time, Demeter was terribly unhappy, and the crops wouldn't grow. But for the rest of the time, Demeter rejoiced, and nature flourished once again.

ARES

God of war

◊ **Ares was the god of the Amazons, and he gave these women their aggressive attitude**, and helped them in their fights. Some Amazon queens were his daughters— Antiope for example, who attacked Athens; Hippolyte, who fought with Heracles; and Penthesilea, who was killed at Troy.

WHERE:
On Mount Olympus or on the battlefield

Ares (Ἄρης) was the Greek god of war and of all the terrors of the battlefield. He was enormously powerful, and his battle cry was as loud as ten thousand warriors all shouting together.

Ares loved fighting for the sake of fighting. He took huge pleasure in the roar of combat, loved killing, and reveled in the devastation of cities. All the other gods hated Ares, but he was extremely handsome, and women adored him.

His most famous partner was the goddess of love, Aphrodite. She was married to Hephaestus, but she and Ares still had lots of children together: Phobos (Fear), Deimos (Terror), Harmonia (Harmony), Eros (Love), and Anteros (Mutual Love). He also had an affair with Eos, the goddess of the dawn.

Enyo, the goddess of war and destruction, gave birth to a son of Ares who they named Enyalius, who was also a war god. A nymph named Harmonia (not his daughter) also fell in love with him and bore him some daughters who all fell in love with fighting—they were the first of the Amazons.

◊ **Ares's sacred animals included a flock of birds who could shoot their feathers like arrows,** and the awesome Colchian Dragon who guarded the Golden Fleece. The Ismenian Dragon, which protected his sacred spring near Thebes, was the offspring of Ares and a Fury named Telphousia.

◊ **Ares was a mighty, bearded warrior who was always equipped for combat.** They called him "Ares of the black spear," but he also carried a sharp sword. He would protect himself with the proper equipment of a Greek warrior—a gleaming helmet, breastplate, greaves (shin armor), and a shield that had ferocious, warlike emblems on it.

GAIA

Primordial goddess of the Earth

> **"** Gaia was constantly fighting with the Olympian gods, and she had a long but unsuccessful contest with Zeus about who should rule the Universe. **"**

WHERE:
The Earth

Gaia (Γαῖα), also known as Gaea or Ge, was the great mother goddess. She was the first power of the earth and fertility, and the parent of all living things—human beings, unreasoning beasts, and senseless plants.

Gaia belonged to the first generation of divinities who came into existence out of Chaos. She then created her equal Ouranos (Sky), to cover her and to be the home of the gods, followed by hills and Pontos (the Sea).

Gaia had children with Ouranos, who were known as the Titans and Titanesses, along with their siblings the Cyclopes (who each had one round eye in the middle of their forehead) and the mighty and violent Hundred-Handers, who each had 50 heads and 100 arms. Her children were a mysterious group of monsters: the three Erinyes (Furies), the Giants, the ash-tree nymphs, the monstrous creature Typhon (also called Typhoeus or Typhaon), the half-woman, half-snake Echidna, Nereus the Old Man of the Sea, the Dog-Headed Men of Africa and India, the cannibal Laestrygonians, the 16-inch-tall black-skinned Pygmies, and the love goddess Aphrodite.

Gaia was constantly fighting with the Olympian gods, and she had a long but unsuccessful contest with Zeus about who should rule the Universe.

◇ **In the Golden Age, the earth was so fertile** that there was no need to plow or plant the fields because Gaia freely gave all her riches to mortals, who were happy to gather wild strawberries on the mountainside, pick cherries and berries, and eat acorns from the oak trees.

◇ Gaia's children the Titans fought the ten-year "Titanomachy" war against Zeus, making the sea roar, the earth rumble, and Heaven groan. When they lost, Gaia told the Giants to attack the Heavens in revenge, but **Zeus also won in this "Gigantomachy," and became the new ruler of the Universe.**

◇ **Gaia nourished all the creatures of the land, sea, and air from her bounteous store.** Through her human beings were blessed with children, fruitful land, rich harvests, and fields full of cattle.

THE MUSES

The goddesses of music, poetry, and the arts

◇ **You can usually recognize the Nine Muses by the things they carry.** Calliope often holds a writing tablet; Clio has a scroll; Erato likes to play the lyre, while Euterpe plays the flute; Melpomene holds a tragic mask, and Thalia has a comic one; Polymnia looks thoughtful; Terpsichore likes to dance; and Urania holds a globe.

◇ Calliope was the Muse of heroic poetry; Clio looked after history; Erato took care of love poetry; Euterpe was the Muse of music; Melpomene was the goddess of tragedy, and Thalia handled comedy; thoughtful Polymnia oversaw sacred poetry, while lively Terpsichore controlled dancing; Urania was the Muse of astronomy.

WHERE:
Pieria near Mount Olympus and Mount Helicon in Greece

The Nine Muses (Μοῦσαι) were the daughters of Zeus and the Titaness Mnemosyne ("Memory"). They were the goddesses of the arts, literature, and science. They were born in Pieria, near the topmost snowy peak of Mount Olympus.

The Muses were beautiful, carefree young women who wore long glamorous robes, and always had their hearts set on singing. They performed at Achilles's funeral and made all the Greek warriors cry.

Poets and singers prayed to them for inspiration. When the great poet Homer wanted to tell the story of the Trojan War, he said to Calliope, "Sing, goddess, the anger of Peleus's son Achilles," and when he started to recite the tale of Odysseus, he asked her, "Tell me, Muse, of the man of many ways, who was driven far journeys, after he had sacked Troy's sacred citadel."

It was very dangerous to challenge the Muses, like Thamyris did. He was very beautiful and a fine musician, and he invited them to have a musical contest with him. When he lost, the Muses took away both his musical talent and his eyesight.

THE FATES

Controllers of destiny

WHERE:
Down in the Underworld or wandering in the night

> Lachesis, the Apportioner of Lots, would measure out how long or short it would be; and Atropos, She Who Cannot Be Turned, who was the shortest, eldest, and most senior of the three goddesses, would then snip it off.

The Fates were called the Moirae (Μοῖραι) in Greek. *Moirae* means parts, shares, or allotted portions, and it was their job to give everybody their "share" of life. They were severe, implacable ancient goddesses who controlled the Fate or Destiny of every human being who ever walked the Earth. They decided how long every single person would be allowed to live.

They wore headbands and white or purple clothes, and worked closely as a team to weave their web of inescapable Destiny. There were three of them: Clotho, the Spinner, would spin the thread of the person's life; Lachesis, the Apportioner of Lots, would measure out how long or short it would be; and Atropos, She Who Cannot Be Turned, who was the shortest, eldest, and most senior of the three goddesses, would then snip it off. That was the moment when the person would die.

PROMETHEUS

A trickster who defied the gods

WHERE:
Deceiving Zeus at Mecone in Greece or chained to Mount Caucasus

Prometheus (Προμηθεύς) was a great trickster. His name means "foresight," and he brought some wonderful benefits to humankind. Some Greeks even said that he created men by molding them out of water and earth. His greatest gift to humans was fire.

Once, when the gods and mortals were dividing up an ox, Prometheus concealed the tasty meat in the stomach of the ox and hid the inedible bones in the delicious-looking fat. Then he invited Zeus to choose a portion. Zeus picked the most delicious-looking bits but was furious when he discovered they were full of bones. As a punishment, Zeus took away fire so man would have to eat meat raw.

But Prometheus got up to his tricks again and stole fire from Zeus by hiding it inside a hollow fennel stalk. Zeus was so angry that he created Pandora, the first woman, to be a balancing evil, and ordered the god of fire, Hephaestus, to chain Prometheus to Mount Caucasus. There a long-winged eagle came and ate his immortal liver, which then grew back every night. After 30,000 years, Prometheus was freed by Heracles, who also shot the great eagle.

◇ **Zeus was in love with the sea goddess Thetis,** but one reason why he allowed Prometheus to be freed was that Prometheus told him a great secret: Thetis was destined to bear a son greater than his father. Zeus decided not to chase after Thetis anymore, and she eventually married Peleus and gave birth to Achilles.

◇ Heracles accidentally shot the friendly Centaur Chiron with one of his arrows that were soaked in the Hydra's deadly poison. The wound was incurable and extremely painful. But Chiron was immortal and even though he wanted to die, he couldn't. **Prometheus offered to become immortal instead of him, and so Chiron died peacefully.**

◇ **Zeus told Prometheus to make humans and animals, but Prometheus made too many animals.** So Zeus ordered him to turn some of the animals into people. Prometheus did as he was told, and so the people who were originally animals all have a human body but the soul of an animal.

PAN

> "He was a lover of merry noise, and liked to dance, even though he was really bad at it!"

God of nature, shepherds, flocks, and of mountain wilds

WHERE:
The ruggedly beautiful countryside of Arcadia

Pan (Πάν) was the countryside god of shepherds, hunters, meadows, forests, mountain peaks, and rocky crests. The Greeks could never make their minds up about who his parents were. Some people said they were Hermes and a nymph named Penelope or Dryops, while others said they were Zeus and Hybris.

His name, Pan, comes from the Greek word for "everything," because he is said to have delighted everyone. He was a strange and uncanny god, who caused panic among people who strayed into his territory. He spent a lot of time with the god of the grape-harvest Dionysus and was said to have taught the god Apollo the art of prophecy.

Pan spent most of his time lazing around playing his panpipes or chasing after nymphs. He was a lover of merry noise, and liked to dance, even though he was really bad at it! He liked to sleep at midday, but in the evening, after he had been out hunting and slaying wild beasts, he would play sweet, low music on his pipes, and sing high-pitched songs. Then the clear-voiced nymphs would join him, singing by quiet springs and dancing on their nimble feet in soft meadows.

◊ **Pan was part-human, part-animal.** He had keen eyes, long messy hair, a bushy beard, a snub nose, and pointy ears, as well as the horns, legs, and tail of a goat. He was covered in hair and was so strange that his mother ran away in fear the first time she saw him.

◊ The nymph Syrinx ran away from Pan but found her escape blocked by a river. She prayed to the river nymphs, and was turned into a reed, which made a beautiful sound in the wind. **Pan loved this sound so he fastened reeds of different lengths together and made the panpipes, which the Greeks called the syrinx.**

◊ Pan also fell in love with Echo, who was a beautiful singer, but when she rejected him, he drove his followers mad, and they tore her to pieces. Gaia, the goddess of the Earth, hid the pieces inside herself, and **Echo's musical voice survived, perfectly imitating the sound of any earthly creature.**

EROS

God of love

WHERE:
Everywhere

Eros (Ἔρως) was the god of love, and was said to be the most beautiful of all the gods. His mother was Aphrodite, and although she had a tough time making him do as he was told, he was extremely loyal to her. Eros was young, pretty, and extremely naughty, but he was also an awesome power of nature.

He loved to play tricks on people and could be very cruel, often acting at random and laughing out loud at the effect he had. No mortal, immortal, or monster was safe from him: he made men and women weak and overpowered even the cleverest minds.

He would make people fall in love using a burning torch or by shooting them with his bow and arrows. Eros could break Zeus's thunderbolts, take Heracles's weapons off him, tame lions and tigers, and play mischievous games with sea creatures. He had two kinds of arrows, sharp golden ones that inspired intense passion, and blunt, heavy ones made out of lead, which caused people to reject their lovers. The Romans called him Cupid or Amor.

◊ **Eros had golden wings and carried his bow and arrows in a golden quiver.** Sometimes he would wear a blindfold, because he often acted blindly. He always had a good supply of love gifts, such as flowers, sashes, or hares.

◊ **If Eros shot you with one of his golden arrows,** speechless amazement would seize you and the arrow would burn deep in your heart like a flame. You would keep staring at the person you loved, your soul would melt with sweet pain, and your cheeks would blush and then go pale.

◊ **Aphrodite ordered Eros to make Psyche (the Soul) fall in love, but Eros fell in love with Psyche instead.** He hid his real identity and told her never to look at his face. She disobeyed him and as a result he rejected her. But after Aphrodite made Psyche do some almost impossible tasks, Eros and Psyche were reunited and got married.

> *She ruled as the queen of Ithaca and waited patiently for 20 years for Odysseus to return from the Trojan War.*

◊ **Penelope was gorgeous, accomplished, intelligent, cunning, and the heiress to a very important kingdom.** When suitors looked at her, they all fell in love. Their knees gave way, their hearts filled with passion, and each one of them prayed that he would one day become her husband.

◊ The big secret that Penelope and her husband shared was about their immovable bed. Odysseus had built it himself, using a live olive tree. Penelope told her maid to bring the bed outside. The bed was extremely precious to the couple, so when Odysseus thought their bed was outdoors, he got angry and wanted to know who had moved it. **His furious reaction confirmed to Penelope that this was definitely her husband.**

PENELOPE

The faithful wife of Odysseus and the mother of Telemachus

WHERE:

In Odysseus's palace on the island of Ithaca

Penelope (**Πηνελόπη or Πηνελόπεια**) was **the cautious, careful, and faithful wife of Odysseus and the mother of Telemachus. She ruled as the queen of Ithaca and waited patiently for 20 years for Odysseus to return from the Trojan War, not knowing if he was alive or dead.**

Men wanted to marry her, but she always hoped that Odysseus would return. She kept them away with a great trick...

During the day, she would weave a shroud for the funeral of Odysseus's father, and the suitors had no choice but to wait until she was finished. But at night she would secretly undo all of her work. But eventually they discovered Penelope's trick.

Odysseus, in disguise, returned just in time and killed all of the suitors. He looked so filthy and disgusting that Penelope didn't recognize him at first. However, they had special secret signs that only the two of them knew, and when they had given these to each other, they truly knew that they were reunited as man and wife. They fell into each other's arms, shedding tears of joy.

◊ **Penelope was very unhappy in Odysseus's long and painful absence.** She would sit, resting her cheek on her hand, sighing and crying all day long. At night she used to lie on her bed of sorrows, soaking it with her tears until she finally fell asleep.

THE ODYSSEY

The Odyssey is the story of how Odysseus got back home to Ithaca after the Trojan War.

He started by **attacking a tribe called the Cicones**, although he spared a priest named Maro, who gave him 12 jars of honey-sweet wine.

Odysseus then sailed to the land of the Lotus-eaters. **Anyone who tasted the fruit of the lotus would forget absolutely everything they'd ever known** and want to stay with the Lotus-eaters forever. Odysseus had to drag some of his crew back to the ships after they ate some.

His travels then brought him to the land of the monstrous, **one-eyed cannibal Cyclops**. After the Cyclops had eaten a few of Odysseus's men, Odysseus encouraged him to drink so much of Maro's wine that he fell fast asleep.

Odysseus then blinded the Cyclops with a sharp wooden stake and escaped from his cave by hiding underneath a ram as the flock walked outside to graze. **The Cyclops cursed Odysseus** when he found out that he wasn't actually called "Nobody," as Odysseus had first told him, but "Odysseus, Sacker of Cities."

Odysseus then traveled to Aeolia, whose king, Aeolus, was the keeper of the winds. Aeolus gave Odysseus **a bag stuffed with all the winds** apart from the West Wind, which blew Odysseus on his way. But when Odysseus could see Ithaca, he fell asleep, and his crew, thinking that the bag was full of treasure, opened it.

The **winds burst out and caused a massive storm** that drove them far away from their homeland.

Odysseus sailed on to the land of the Laestrygonians, who were cannibal Giants. Tens of thousands of them swarmed down to the sea, throwing **man-sized boulders and eating the sailors** when they got their hands on them.

Odysseus sailed away with **the only ship he had left** and put it on Circe's island. She was a witch who turned some of Odysseus's sailors into pigs. The god of trade, Hermes, gave Odysseus some antidotes so that he could make his men human again, and then he stayed with Circe for a whole year.

His next adventure was a "calling-up of the ghosts," in which he tried three times to embrace his mother's soul. But three times she fluttered out of his hands. In the end, fear got the better of Odysseus, and **he sailed on, past the Sirens and their dangerous**

singing, **past the dog-headed snaky sea monster Scylla**, who ate six of his sailors alive, and on to Thrinacia, where his crew stupidly slaughtered the oxen of the sun.

Zeus blasted this last ship with a thunderbolt, and all the crew were lost, **leaving Odysseus alone, clinging onto the wreckage**. He narrowly **escaped the whirlpool of Charybdis** and was washed ashore on the nymph Calypso's island, where he spent seven years. She offered him immortality if he would stay, but in the end, **he wanted to go home to Ithaca to his wife, Penelope**.

But his journey wasn't over yet! He had to be rescued from another storm by the White Goddess and Athena, and he swam ashore to the island of the Phaeacians. There, looking a complete mess, he met the princess Nausicaa, who took him home to meet

her parents in their wondrous palace. He told them his story, and **one of their ships brought him home to Ithaca**.

There he met his old dog, who immediately died happy, his son Telemachus, his friend Eumaeus, and his old nurse Eurycleia. **He strung his old bow, shot all the suitors who had been pestering Penelope**, and was happily reunited with his faithful wife. They talked, she of her troubles, he of his travels, until sweet sleep overtook them.

NARCISSUS

A hunter known for his staggering beauty

WHERE:
In the pathless woods of the mountains of Boeotia in Greece

Narcissus (Νἀρκισσος) **was one of the most beautiful young men who ever lived. He had eyes like stars, exquisite fingers, magnificent flowing hair, cheeks that were youthful and smooth, an elegant neck that looked like ivory, and a complexion as fair as a rose petal. Countless girls, boys, and nymphs all fell in love with him, but he rejected them all.**

A nymph named Echo was besotted with him, but he was horrible to her. "Keep your hands off me!" he said. "Get away! I'll die before I yield to you." She was heartbroken and went away to a lonely mountain cave, where she dissolved into nothing but an empty voice.

When a youth named Ameinias was also cruelly rejected by Narcissus, he killed himself outside Narcissus's door. So Nemesis, the goddess who punishes self-importance, arranged that one very hot day, as Narcissus was leaning over a pool to take a drink, he saw his own face reflected in the water. He instantly fell passionately in love with himself. But however hard Narcissus tried to kiss and embrace his reflection, it always disappeared when he touched the water.

He stayed by the pool, yearning for himself, and pined away until he died.

" **He instantly fell passionately in love with himself.** "

◇ Some say that **as Narcissus gazed longingly at his own image in the pool** he slowly faded away, and the nymphs transformed him into a narcissus flower. Others say that he was filled with remorse and killed himself, and it was from his blood that the flower was born.

◇ Echo was a strange-voiced nymph who had been cursed so that **she could only speak if someone else spoke first.** All she could do was repeat the last word that was said, and echo back the voice that she'd heard: when Narcissus shouted, "Is anyone here?" she called back, "Here!"

◇ Narcissus was a hunter who used nets to catch animals on the wild mountains. It was in the midday heat when he lay down in the shade beside a bright, glassy, silver-clear spring, surrounded by sweet grasses and trees, **and saw his own fateful reflection.**

OEDIPUS

Greek king of Thebes

WHERE:
On Mount Cithaeron, then at Corinth, and finally at Thebes in Greece

King Laius of Thebes was warned by an oracle that his son would kill him. But nonetheless he and his wife, Jocasta, eventually had a baby boy named Oedipus (Οἰδίπους). Terrified that the prophecy might come true, they abandoned the baby on Mount Cithaeron, but a shepherd rescued him and gave him to Polybus and Merope, the childless king and queen of Corinth.

They brought him up as their own son, but when Oedipus received an oracle that he would kill his father and marry his mother, thinking that meant Polybus and Merope, he decided to leave Corinth.

On his journey, he killed King Laius in a road-rage incident at a crossroads.

He carried on his journey and ended up at Thebes, which was guarded by the Sphinx. She had a special riddle and devoured anyone who got the answer wrong. Oedipus guessed the answer correctly, and the Sphinx died. He was rewarded by becoming king of Thebes and marrying the widowed Queen Jocasta. Not knowing that they were mother and son, they lived happily together and had four children...until the truth came out. Jocasta killed herself, and Oedipus blinded himself using the dress pins from Jocasta's clothing, before going into exile. Oedipus was eventually swallowed into the earth.

◇ **When he was traveling**, Oedipus wore sandals, a wide-brimmed hat, tunic, and a cloak, and carried a staff.

◇ The riddle of the Sphinx was: **"What is it that has one voice and yet becomes four-footed and two-footed, and three-footed?"** The answer was man. As a baby he crawls "four-footed," as an adult he stands "two-footed," and as an old man with a walking stick, he is "three-footed."

◇ Oedipus became a celebrity after he solved the Sphinx's riddle: **"You all know me, the world knows my fame: I am Oedipus."**

PANDORA

The first human woman created by the gods

WHERE:
Mecone in Greece

When Prometheus ("Foresight") stole fire from Zeus, Zeus wanted to punish the human race: the result of this was Pandora (Πανδώρα), the first woman. She was, "an evil thing for man's delight, and they all loved this ruin in their hearts."

Several forces gathered together to create the first woman. Hephaestus made her out of earth and water, giving her a face like a goddess, and the figure of a young girl; Athena dressed her in exquisite garments, and taught her the art of weaving; Aphrodite poured charm upon her head, but also painful desire and body-shattering cares; Persuasion and the Graces gave her golden necklaces; the Seasons wove spring flowers into a crown for her; Hermes added lies, manipulative words, and cunning ways, and named her Pandora ("Allgift").

Hermes took Pandora to Epimetheus ("Hindsight," Prometheus's stupid brother), who forgot Prometheus's advice to send back any gift from Zeus, in case it should injure humans. Pandora took a jar with her that contained all the evils in the world. Epimetheus made the terrible mistake of accepting Pandora, and then it was too late: she opened the jar and the evils escaped into the world, leaving only Hope, who didn't fly away, under the lid of the jar.

◇ **Nowadays people often talk about Pandora's Box, but she doesn't have a "box" in Greek.** She has a huge pottery storage jar called a pithos. It was big and strong enough to hold all the thousands of troubles that now wander the Earth and bring pain and sorrow to humans.

◇ Pandora was unbelievably pretty, and sometimes looked quite shy. But she was very dangerous to men. She wore the most amazing clothes. **Her silvery outfits included an embroidered veil, garlands of flowers and new-grown herbs, and a crown of gold.**

◇ **What is the meaning of the story?** Some believe that there is no hope for humankind, because Hope herself is shut up in Pandora's pithos. While others think that we at least have hope, if nothing else.

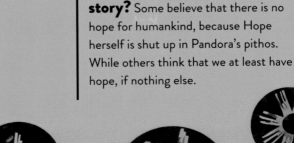

ICARUS

The son of a master craftsman, who flew too close to the sun

" But Icarus was a foolish and annoying child, and the thrill of flying went to his head. "

WHERE:
Crete

After King Minos of Crete discovered that the hero Theseus had escaped from the Labyrinth after killing the Minotaur, he was furious. He imprisoned Daedalus (who'd made the Labyrinth) and Daedalus's son Icarus (Ἴκαρος) inside the Labyrinth as punishment.

◆ The wings that Icarus wore were made from feathers that were cleverly arranged in order, from small to large. The middle feathers were tied with thread, and the lower parts were glued together with wax. **They were arranged in gentle curves, just like those of the birds.**

But Daedalus was very clever and came up with a plan to escape...

He made some wings and showed Icarus how to use them. "Listen carefully!" he said, "Keep to the middle way. If you fly too low, the water will clog your wings; if you fly too high, they'll be scorched by fire. Fly between sea and sun." Like a bird leading its chicks from the nest, Daedalus tried to keep an eye on Icarus as he flew, encouraging and instructing him.

But Icarus was a foolish and annoying child, and the thrill of flying went to his head.

He ignored his father's instructions and soared higher and higher, until the scorching rays of the sun melted the wax that fastened his feathers together. The wax dissolved, and the feathers fell away. Icarus flapped his bare arms and kept shouting, "Father!" but he plummeted down into the blue-green waters of the sea. The area where he fell was called the Icarian Sea.

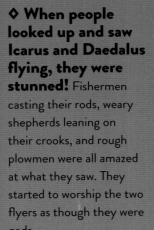

◆ **When people looked up and saw Icarus and Daedalus flying, they were stunned!** Fishermen casting their rods, weary shepherds leaning on their crooks, and rough plowmen were all amazed at what they saw. They started to worship the two flyers as though they were gods.

◆ **Heracles found the body of Icarus washed up on the shore of the island of Doliche.** He buried it and renamed the island Icaria after him. Daedalus honored Heracles by making a statue of him that was so realistic that Heracles threw a stone at it because he thought it was alive.

MIDAS

The king who turned everything he touched to gold

WHERE:
Phrygia, in what is now western-central Turkey

Midas (Μίδας) was the ruler of Phrygia, and always seemed to make the wrong choice. His career started well: when a drunken old man was brought to him as a prisoner, he recognized that he was the god Dionysus's companion, Silenus. Midas entertained him and sent him back to Dionysus, so Dionysus granted Midas one wish.

Without thinking it through, he asked that everything he touched be turned to gold. His delight at being able to transform sticks and stones into precious metal soon turned to horror when the same thing happened to his food and drink. Starving and thirsty, he begged Dionysus to take away this ill-fated gift. The god obliged, telling him to wash in the River Pactolus, which has contained golden sand ever since.

Midas then made another terrible decision. Apollo and Pan were having a musical contest. The mountain god Tmolus was the referee, and he judged that Apollo and his lyre were better than Pan and his pipes. But Midas challenged the decision. In his fury at Midas's total lack of musical appreciation, Apollo transformed his ears into those of a donkey—long, twitching, gray, and bristly.

◊ Midas tried to hide his donkey ears by wearing a "Phrygian cap," rather like a turban. But, of course, his barber saw them. The barber had to tell the astonishing secret to someone, so he dug a hole and whispered the truth into it. Eventually some reeds grew in the hole, and they started to repeat the barber's words (and they still do): **"Midas has donkeys ears."**

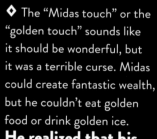

◊ The "Midas touch" or the "golden touch" sounds like it should be wonderful, but it was a terrible curse. Midas could create fantastic wealth, but he couldn't eat golden food or drink golden ice. **He realized that his gift was really a curse, and developed a deep hatred for gold.**

◊ **Silenus was the oldest and wisest of all Dionysus's followers.** He was mostly human, with a potbelly, snub nose, bald head, high forehead, and beard, but he also had a bushy horse's tail and pointy ears. Silenus staggered around naked, drinking and partying, using a hump-backed donkey to help himself stand up.

> **" The curse meant that she could keep the gift of prophecy, but no one would ever believe her. "**

CASSANDRA

Princess of Troy

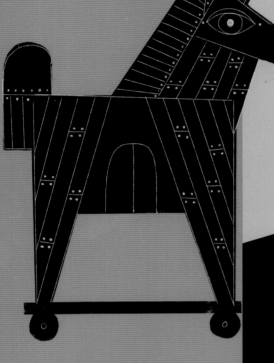

◇ **Cassandra knew what would happen if the Trojans accepted the Wooden Horse.** But no one listened to her. They dragged it into the city, bringing terror and destruction upon themselves.

◇ **Cassandra's power of prophecy was a curse to her for the rest of her life.** It was a terrible thing to have lips that told of a future that the Trojans never believed.

◇ Cassandra always wore the most incredible clothes. As a Trojan princess, she dressed in rich robes and fabulous jewelry. As a strange, uncanny priestess, she would use makeup, body painting, tattooing, and piercing **to create her aura of wild mystery.**

WHERE:
Cassandra lived at Troy and died at Mycenae

Cassandra (Κασσάνδρα) was the daughter of Priam, the king of Troy, and his wife, Hecuba. She was both a princess and a priestess. She was strikingly beautiful and very clever, but when she started predicting the future, everyone just thought she was mad.

The god Apollo fell in love with Cassandra and promised to teach her the art of prophecy if she loved him in return. She accepted the offer, acquired the powers, but failed to deliver her part of the bargain: she did not love him.

Apollo was incredibly angry that she had betrayed him, so he cursed her by kissing her and spitting into her mouth. The curse meant that she could keep the gift of prophecy, but no one would ever believe her, even though she always spoke the truth.

No one believed anything she predicted...She knew that her brother Paris would destroy Troy. She begged her parents to kill him. But they didn't. She warned the Trojans not to take the Wooden Horse into the city. But they did. She was taken prisoner by Agamemnon when the Greeks conquered Troy and was taken back to Mycenae. There she predicted her own death, but everyone thought she was crazy. But she knew the truth, and in the end, she was murdered by Agamemnon's jealous wife, Clytemnestra.

◇ Orpheus wore long musicians' robes and a special cap when he was performing his magical music. **His favorite instrument was the seven-stringed lyre**, which he sometimes played with his fingers, or sometimes with an ivory plectrum. After he died, his instrument was placed in the stars as the constellation Lyra.

ORPHEUS

A legendary musician, poet, and prophet

WHERE:

In Thrace or in the Underworld

Orpheus (Ὀρφεύς) was such an amazing musician that humans, animals, and even the trees and rocks would dance to his melody. When Orpheus's wife, Eurydice, died after a snake bite, he decided to go down to the Underworld and bring her back. He used the power of his music to charm Cerberus the watchdog and Charon the ferryman into letting him in, and persuaded Hades and Persephone to allow him to take Eurydice back to the world above.

But there was one condition...Orpheus had to lead the way, and he mustn't turn around until he had left the realms of the dead.

Orpheus and his wife followed the steep upward slope in deadly silence, all the while surrounded in darkness and mist. When Orpheus saw the exit to Earth and light ahead of him, he began to worry that Eurydice might not be behind him anymore. He looked back, and Eurydice instantly started to disappear into the darkness. She stretched out her arms toward him and struggled to hold his hands. But it was too late. She was gone, and he would never be able to return to the Underworld while he was still alive.

◇ **Orpheus was one of the Argonauts, and he saved them from the music of the Sirens.** These monsters used to enchant whoever sailed close to their island with their sweet but deadly songs, but Orpheus played his own more powerful music on his lyre and overcame the Sirens' singing.

◇ Orpheus died by being torn into pieces by Maenads. Each of these women wanted Orpheus for herself, and their tugging at him ended in his death. **His head floated, still singing, down a river and across the sea to Lesbos. His ghost was happily reunited with his beloved Eurydice.**

HELEN

The most beautiful woman in the world

◊ No description could possibly do justice to Helen's beauty. **There had never been a woman as exquisite as her.** People said she was "just like a goddess," "awe-inspiring," "white-armed," "lovely," and "far surpassed all other mortals in beauty."

◊ **Everyone who saw Helen was amazed by her beauty.** When the old men of Troy looked at her in admiration, they understood why the Greeks and the Trojans fought for such a long time in the Trojan War and suffered such hardships to win her.

> The "face that launched a thousand ships," the most beautiful woman in the world, who caused the greatest war of all time.

WHERE:
Sparta, then Troy, then back in Sparta

Helen (Ἑλένη), often known as the "face that launched a thousand ships," was the daughter of Zeus, when he was in the form of a swan, and Leda, the wife of King Tyndareus of Sparta. Helen's astonishing beauty attracted countless Greek leaders who all wanted to marry her.

Tyndareus made all the suitors swear an oath to provide military assistance to the winning suitor in case Helen was ever led astray.

Menelaus was the successful suitor, but it wasn't a trouble-free relationship and it wasn't long before a Trojan prince named Paris stole Helen from him...

Paris sailed to Sparta, ran away with Helen, and took her back to Troy. The Greek kings were reminded of the oath they took to always help the winning suitor, and 43 chieftains embarked with their men in 1,106 ships and sailed for Troy to get her back. When the Greeks conquered Troy after ten years of fighting, Menelaus was going to kill Helen, but when he saw again how gorgeous she was, he dropped his sword, and they returned to Sparta together.

◊ **The Greeks couldn't make up their minds about what Helen did.** Was she evil? Was it the irresistible power of persuasion? Did Paris carry her off by force? Did she go willingly? Or maybe it wasn't even Helen that Paris abducted, but a phantom version of her made out of clouds?

◊ Achilles was a young, beardless warrior who had long reddish-golden, flame-colored hair. His armor included a shield with wondrous scenes of war and peace carved on it. **His awesome ash-wood spear was so huge, heavy, and thick that no one else could use it.**

ACHILLES

The best Greek warrior in the Trojan War

WHERE:
Troy and its battlefield

◊ Achilles was educated by the good Centaur Chiron, who fed him on the entrails of lions and wild boars and the marrows of bears, fawns, and deer. **This gave him the strength and courage of the savage animals and the quickness of the timid ones.**

◊ **Thetis foresaw that Achilles would die at Troy, so to protect him, she dressed him in female clothing and hid him among the women on Scyros.** But Odysseus discovered him by showing the group baskets of jewelry with weapons hidden among them. While the women admired the jewels, Achilles couldn't resist the weapons and grabbed them—thus revealing himself.

Achilles (Ἀχιλλεύς) was the leader of the Myrmidons and was the finest of all the Greek warriors at Troy. He was the son of King Peleus and the sea nymph Thetis. His mother wanted to make him immortal, so holding him by the heel, she dipped him in the River Styx in order to make him totally invulnerable. But there was one bit she missed—the spot where she held him. This was known as his "Achilles heel."

Achilles took 50 ships to Troy and was joined by his best friend, Patroclus. However, Patroclus was murdered by a mighty Trojan hero named Hector.

This enraged Achilles, and he took to the battlefield, fighting warrior after warrior. He took out so many Trojans that he clogged up the River Scamander with their bodies, before finally killing Hector in revenge.

He refused to give Hector's body back until Hector's old father, Priam, visited him in his tent and persuaded him to release it. Achilles then kept on battling and killed Memnon, king of the Ethiopians, and Penthesilea, queen of the Amazons. But one fateful day as he was pursuing some Trojan warriors, he was hit by an arrow shot by Paris, which pierced his one vulnerable spot—his heel—and killed him.

HECTOR

A Trojan prince and epic fighter

WHERE:
Troy—on the battlefield, or in an intimate domestic setting with his family

Hector (Ἕκτωρ), the eldest son of Priam and Hecuba, was Troy's greatest warrior. He was married to Andromache and together they had a baby named Astyanax. He gave everything for his family and city.

Hector "of the shining helmet" was a horse-taming, godlike warrior. But he wasn't a mindless fighting machine—he was a good son and a loving husband and father who shared tender moments with his wife and their baby son.

When he killed Achilles's best friend, Patroclus, Achilles wanted revenge. Achilles was younger and stronger, and Hector knew that he would lose if they fought. But his honor made him fight anyway.

At a crucial moment in their battle, he lost his nerve and made a desperate dash for safety. Achilles chased him three times around the walls of Troy. Athena appeared to Hector and persuaded him to stand his ground. But she soon disappeared, and Hector was left alone to defend himself.

Up on Mount Olympus, Zeus used a pair of golden scales to weigh the fates of the two men. Hector's was heavier and his last hope, Apollo his protector, deserted him. Hector was no match for Achilles, and he went down fighting.

◇ **Hector was a mighty, noble, good-looking Trojan warrior.** Before he fought Achilles, he had two huge fights with the hero Great Ajax. The first lasted all day and ended in a draw. The second was in the Greek camp, and although Hector was wounded by a massive rock, he managed to disarm Ajax, but not to kill him.

◇ When Andromache was upset because Hector had to go back into battle, he stroked her with his hand and told her that he could not bear the thought of her being captured by the invading Greeks and taken into slavery. **He would rather be dead than hear her being dragged away into captivity.**

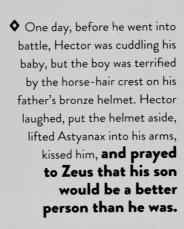

◇ One day, before he went into battle, Hector was cuddling his baby, but the boy was terrified by the horse-hair crest on his father's bronze helmet. Hector laughed, put the helmet aside, lifted Astyanax into his arms, kissed him, **and prayed to Zeus that his son would be a better person than he was.**

THE TROJAN WAR

The Trojan War was fought when Greece's mightiest warriors battled for ten years against Troy's awesome fighters to win back the most beautiful woman who ever lived.

At the wedding of Peleus and Thetis, Eris (Strife), who hadn't been invited, **threw a golden apple among the guests**. The apple had the words "for the fairest" written on it, and Hera, Athena, and Aphrodite each claimed that the prize should be theirs. To put an end to their squabbles, Zeus ordered Hermes to take them to the Trojan prince Paris, who would have to decide.

Aphrodite promised to give Paris the most beautiful woman on Earth, Helen, if he chose her. He did—and when he stole Helen from her husband, King Menelaus, and took her to Troy, this caused the Trojan War.

King Menelaus's brother Agamemnon put together a Greek **army of 1,106 ships** to get her back from Paris. Agamemnon had to sacrifice his daughter Iphigenia to get favorable winds for his army of ships. **The battle raged for years and years**, and in the tenth year, Agamemnon had a huge row with Achilles over some captured girls. Because of this row, Achilles stormed off to his tent in a heroic sulk and **refused to fight**.

Achilles's temper tantrum gave Troy's greatest warrior Hector time to take his ferocious onslaught right into the Greek camp. **Achilles's best friend, Patroclus, borrowed his fabulous armor** and led his troops to save the ships from this attack, but he was no match for Hector, who **killed him in a ferocious battle**.

Achilles was distraught at the news that his friend had died. His mother, Thetis, and his horse Xanthus—who could see into the future—both told him that he would **die almost immediately if he took revenge on Hector,** but he ignored them both. He got some incredible new armor, ended his feud with Agamemnon, and rejoined the battle.

Even the gods got involved this time—all fighting to win this battle that had raged for years. **The Trojans were driven inside the city,** except for Hector. He tried to run for safety, but "swift-footed" Achilles chased him around Troy's walls three times before killing him in single combat.

After his victory over Hector, Achilles returned to the fray, but was **killed by Paris, who shot an arrow at him that struck his heel**. With their finest fighter lost, the Greeks needed Odysseus's cunning to get possession of a statue of Athena called **the Palladium**. While it was inside the walls, Troy could not be captured.

Odysseus had a brilliant idea: **the Wooden Horse**. On the outside was an inscription saying it was an offering to Athena from the Greeks for their return home, but inside the Horse were some mighty Greek fighters...

The rest of the Greek army set sail and the Trojans thought the invaders had gone for good. Despite a warning from their priest Laocoön telling them to "beware of Greeks bearing gifts," they joyfully dragged the Horse into their city.

When night fell, the Greek army, who had pretended to sail away, came back. **Meanwhile the warriors leaped from the Horse** and opened the city gates, letting their fellow soldiers in. The Greeks murdered the sleeping people of Troy and **destroyed the whole city**. King Menelaus led Helen back to the ships, away from Troy, and they sailed away as the city burned behind them.

THE AMAZONS

A tribe of aggressive female warriors

◇ There were some terrifying African Amazons who used the skins of huge snakes for armor. They conquered all the cities on the island of Hespera, apart from where the Ethiopian "Fish-Eaters" lived. Then they subdued the very civilized Atlanteans, and their neighbors the Gorgons. **They were eventually destroyed by Heracles, because he didn't think people should be ruled by women**.

◇ **Theseus captured the Amazon queen, Antiope, and they had a boy child named Hippolytus**. The rest of the warrior women invaded Athens to try to get Antiope back, and when Theseus later rejected Antiope and married Phaedra, the Amazons turned up at the wedding and threatened to kill all of the guests. The Amazons were defeated, though, and Antiope was killed.

◇ The exquisitely beautiful Amazon queen Penthesilea **fought bravely on the Trojan side against the Greeks at Troy**. In the end, she was overpowered by Achilles's superior might, but as he thrust his spear into her body, their eyes met, and for one beautiful but tragic moment, they fell in love.

WHERE:
They lived at Themiscyra at the mouth of the River Thermodon, at the very eastern edge of the Greek world

The Amazons were a race of mighty warriors who hunted with swift, keen-scenting hounds. They were beautiful, athletic, and loved to wear colorful, flamboyant, Persian-style clothes and hats. Jazzy zigzag or harlequin-patterned trousers and tunics were always popular, even when they were going to war.

They used lots of different kinds of armor and helmets and were experts in combat. They could fight at long range with their bows and arrows, or eye-to-eye with their spears and shields. Some of them fought on horseback, and the wars they waged were so famous that the Greeks even had a special word for an Amazon-fight—"Amazonomachy."

The Amazons were haters of men and killed any who got in their way. But they also behaved like men and admired manly virtues. On the few occasions they had babies, they only brought up the girls and gave the boys away.

" The Amazons were haters of men and killed any who got in their way. **"**

JASON

The hero who went in search of the Golden Fleece

WHERE:
From Greece to Colchis on the Black Sea and back

Jason (Ἰάσων) was the most handsome hero who ever lived and led the Argonauts in their quest to get the Golden Fleece. It was because of his beauty that the sorceress Medea agreed to help him steal the Fleece from her own father, Aeetes. Medea **fell deeply in love with Jason and gave him potions that made him invincible.**

In order to get the Golden Fleece, Jason had to attach a plow to two fearsome bronze-footed, fire-breathing bulls that belonged to Aeetes. He then had to plow an enormous field, sowing the teeth of a terrifying serpent. The teeth quickly grew into armed warriors, but Jason managed to defeat them by hurling a huge boulder at them. Despite all this, Aeetes still wouldn't give Jason the Fleece.

Medea offered to lull the Fleece's guardian serpent to sleep, if Jason agreed to marry her. Jason agreed, and so Medea sprinkled the monster's eyes with her mysterious potion and chanted her song. The serpent stretched out into a deep slumber, and Jason grabbed the Golden Fleece.

But once back in Greece, Jason decided to marry someone else. Medea was furious and in her rage destroyed his new wife with her magic and murdered the children she'd had with Jason. The broken-hearted Jason was killed by a rotting beam that fell off his ship, the *Argo*.

◊ Jason was wonderfully beautiful. Never before had anyone seen a hero like this. People gasped as he walked through the crowds, **his comrades looked in wonder at his graceful radiance, and women fell instantly in love with him.**

◊ **Jason had a gorgeous cloak embroidered by Athena**. It showed Cyclopes making thunderbolts; Amphion and Zethus building Thebes; Aphrodite making herself beautiful; a terrible fight over some oxen; the chariot race between Pelops and Oenomaus; Apollo shooting down the monstrous Tityus; and Phrixus, listening to the ram with the Golden Fleece.

◊ The Golden Fleece was made from the wondrous wool of a golden, winged ram. **It shone like a cloud blushing red with the beams of the rising sun.** Aeetes kept it in a grove of Ares, with its guardian serpent writhing in front of it, hissing hideously, and watching it with his keen, sleepless eyes.

MEDEA

A sorceress from Colchis who helped Jason get the Golden Fleece

◇ **To destroy Creon's daughter Glauce, Medea sent her a gown and a coronet (a type of small crown) as a present.** But they were soaked in magical poison. When Glauce put it on, the coronet caught fire, while the dress melted on her skin.

◇ Medea came from Colchis on the Black Sea. She was beautiful and exotic, but she was also a terrifying barbarian princess— and sorceress. **She could be a sweet young girl in love, but she was a monstrous destroyer of anyone who got in her way.**

◇ When Medea killed an ancient ram and plunged it into a boiling cauldron full of her potions, a newborn lamb emerged and friskily scampered away. When Medea persuaded the daughters of the king of Iolcus, Pelias, that they could rejuvenate their old father in the same way, **it just resulted in his horrifyingly painful death**.

> **Medea gave Jason advice and potions and cast spells that helped him win the Golden Fleece.**

WHERE:
From Colchis on the Black Sea, to Iolcus and then Corinth in Greece

Medea (Μήδεια) was the niece of the witch Circe, and the daughter of King Aeetes of Colchis, owner the Golden Fleece.

When the dazzlingly beautiful Jason arrived in search of the Golden Fleece, the god of love Eros shot Medea with an arrow, causing her to fall hopelessly in love with him. But she was a powerful sorceress, and she held the key to Jason's success, and eventually his downfall...

Medea gave Jason advice and potions and cast spells that helped him win the Golden Fleece. Then the pair eloped and got married on their journey back to Greece. On the way, Medea murdered her own brother Apsyrtus and threw him into the sea to distract and delay those that were trying to chase after her.

When she arrived in Jason's hometown of Iolcus, Medea destroyed Pelias, the king who had sent Jason to get the Fleece, using her powerful magic. She and Jason then fled to Corinth, had children, and lived happily ever after... until Jason decided to marry Glauce, the daughter of King Creon of Corinth. Medea was furious and killed Glauce. And to make sure that she devastated Jason completely, she killed their children and flew away in a chariot drawn by dragons.

THE ARGONAUTS

The Argonauts were a group of Greece's most amazing heroes, who sailed in a ship called the *Argo* with Jason, in the quest of the Golden Fleece.

King Pelias of Iolcus had laid claim to his throne by imprisoning any rivals and heirs. But then he received an oracle telling him to beware of the man with a single sandal.

While crossing a river one day, his nephew **Jason lost one of his sandals**. When King Pelias saw him, he was sure his prophecy was about to become true. Worried that Jason would overthrow him, Pelias sent Jason far away to fetch the Golden Fleece. Jason accepted the challenge to track down the Fleece so that he would then be able to claim his inheritance and throne.

The Fleece was in Colchis on the Black Sea and was guarded by a sleepless dragon, so King Pelias assumed that Jason wouldn't return from this seemingly impossible quest.

Jason's ship, the *Argo*, was made from speaking timber and the crew, **the Argonauts ("Argo-sailors"), were a collection of Greece's finest heroes**. The first stop on their journey was at the island of Lemnos, which was inhabited by man-hating women. However, Jason was so beautiful that their princess Hypsipyle fell in love with him, and the Argonauts were allowed to stay awhile.

Next, they journeyed to the land of the Doliones, where King Cyzicus received them kindly. However, when powerful winds drove the *Argo* back to his territory, **he thought the Argonauts were pirates**, and tried to fight them off. Tragically, Jason killed him.

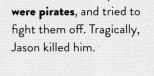

Farther along their journey, the Argonauts entered into a rowing competition. **Heracles made the Argo travel so fast** that the ship almost fell apart! The Argonauts then accidentally left him behind while Heracles was looking for his boyfriend, Hylas, who had been abducted by some water nymphs.

Jason and his men journeyed on and on, meeting many dangers and obstacles. They traveled through the **land of the Amazons**, meeting strange tribes and fending off an attack by birds that used their feathers as arrows, until they arrived in Colchis. As Jason walked into King Aeetes's amazing palace, **his sorceress daughter Medea fell completely in love**. She helped Jason perform incredible feats of heroism.

However, her father still wouldn't give Jason the Golden Fleece, and so **Medea sedated the serpent** that guarded it so Jason could grab it.

They sailed for home, pursued by Medea's family, but Jason and his men managed to defeat them and escaped. They **sailed past the Sirens**, thanks to the musical prowess of Orpheus, whose singing neutralized the power of their song. They **passed the cliff of Scylla** and the **seething roar of the sea monster, Charybdis**. They then **navigated through the Wandering Rocks** with the help of some sea nymphs. Eventually they reached the Island of the Cattle of the Sun, and soon **Jason and Medea made their marriage official**.

A storm then blew them to Syrtis, where sand stretched as far as the eye could see, until **a tsunami drove the Argo so far inland that they had to carry the ship on their shoulders** to Lake Tritonis. From there the god Triton helped get the Argo back into the Mediterranean Sea.

As they approached Crete, **Medea used her magic to destroy the bronze Giant Talos**, after which the Argonauts sped safely back to where they started. Jason, ready to reclaim his throne, gave King Pelias the Golden Fleece, but because King Pelias had killed Jason's family while he was away, Medea took vengeance on him by tricking his daughters into boiling him alive.

CYCLOPS

A monster with a single eye on his forehead

WHERE:
A cave on an island, quite close to the sea, with pasture lands outside

Polyphemus (Πολύφημος) the Cyclops (Κύκλωψ) was a monstrous Giant with one eye in the middle of his forehead.

One day, while Polyphemus was out with his sheep, Odysseus and his 12 companions wandered into his empty cave. But Polyphemus soon came back with his flock of sheep and rolled a massive stone across the entrance behind him. Odysseus and his men were trapped and quickly hid. But Polyphemus knew there was someone in his cave…

"Who are you, strangers?" he yelled. Odysseus crept out from his hiding place and shouted, "My name is Nobody." By way of reply, Polyphemus grabbed two men and ate them. In the morning, before he went out with his sheep, Polyphemus ate two more men. He rolled the giant stone back in place and left Odysseus and the remaining men sealed in his cave.

When he returned, Odysseus offered him some wine. Polyphemus gulped it down quickly and fell fast asleep. When Odysseus was completely sure that Polyphemus was asleep, he heated up a long stake of olive wood in the fire. With a great heave, he and his men drove the stake into the monster's one eye and blinded him.

When Polyphemus screamed for help, his neighbors asked who was hurting him. "Nobody!" he roared, and so they all went away. Odysseus and his remaining companions tied themselves underneath the blind Cyclops's sheep, and when he let them out in the morning, he frisked the sheep's backs but missed the men underneath. Odysseus and his men were free! They stole the sheep and sailed away.

◊ When Odysseus escaped from the Cyclops's cave, he hurled insults at the monster. Polyphemus threw a massive rock at him, which almost wrecked Odysseus's ship. Then Odysseus told him his true identity, **"You were blinded by Odysseus the Sacker of Cities. His father is Laertes. His home is in Ithaca!"**

◊ **When the Cyclops grabbed the first of Odysseus's companions,** he caught them both together and decided they would be his first meal. He cut them up limb by limb and ate them, entrails, flesh, and bones alike, without leaving a single crumb.

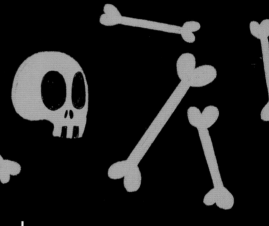

◊ Cyclopes were totally uncivilized. They had no laws or settled customs and they lived in caves without any concern for their neighbours. **They didn't care about Zeus and the Olympian gods, because they thought they were better than them.**

ARGOS

> He had 100 starlike
> eyes all over his head
> and body. "

A hundred-eyed Giant

WHERE:
In the woods, pastures, and mountains around the city of Argos in Greece

Argos (Ἄργος) was an enormous monster who the Greeks called "Panoptes," which means "All-seeing." He had 100 starlike eyes all over his head and body. The eyes took turns to rest, two at a time, while all the others stayed watchful and awake.

He is best known as the guardian of Io, who was a staggeringly beautiful priestess of Hera. Hera's husband, Zeus, loved Io and changed her into striking white heifer to hide the relationship from his wife. But Hera wasn't fooled. She never was. She cunningly asked Zeus to give her the cow as a present, and then ordered Argos to guard the animal-girl.

Io was able to write her name (the two letters iota and omega: IΩ) in the dust with her hoof, to tell her father what had happened, but Argos just moved her somewhere else. In the end, Zeus got Hermes to disguise himself as a shepherd and lull Argos to sleep with the divine music of his panpipes.

As soon as Argos started to nod off, Hermes struck him with his curved sword, right where the head joined the neck, and sent it rolling down a steep cliff, staining the rocks with Argos's blood.

◊ **Argos was unbelievably strong.** He once killed a raging bull and then used its hide as a cloak; he slew the cattle thief Satyrus; and he got rid of Echidna, who used to kidnap travelers.

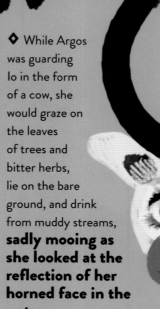

◊ While Argos was guarding Io in the form of a cow, she would graze on the leaves of trees and bitter herbs, lie on the bare ground, and drink from muddy streams, **sadly mooing as she looked at the reflection of her horned face in the water.**

> *It was bred in the swamp of Lerna, where it terrorized the local countryside.*

◇ **The Hydra's close relatives were some of the most fearsome Greek monsters,** such as the fire-breathing Chimera, multi-headed Cerberus, the Nemean Lion, the Sphinx, the Colchian Dragon that guarded the Golden Fleece, Ladon the Hesperian Dragon, the two-headed dog Orthrus, and the great eagle that ate Prometheus's liver.

THE HYDRA

A many-headed serpent

◇ **The Hydra was so poisonous** that she could kill people just by breathing on them, even when she was asleep.

◇ **The swamp of Lerna was close to one of the entrances of the Underworld.** Sometimes the Hydra could be found hissing horribly by the doors of Hades alongside the monstrous forms of other beasts such as the Centaurs, Scylla, the Hundred-Hander Briareus, the fire-breathing Chimaera, the Gorgons and Harpies, and three-bodied Geryon.

WHERE:
In the swamp of Lerna in Greece, and in the Underworld

The Hydra (Ὕδρα) was a monstrous, poisonous water-serpent with a huge body and multiple snake heads, of which the middle one was immortal. Its parents were the semi-human she-dragon Echidna and the storm-giant Typhon.

The Hydra was bred in the swamp of Lerna, where it terrorized the local countryside, raiding the flocks and ruining the land. The goddess Hera nurtured it. She hated the hero Heracles, and his second Labor was to kill it. He flushed it out of its lair with blazing arrows. It coiled itself around his feet, and although he kept hitting its heads with his club, this only made things worse. The moment one head was destroyed, two more grew up in its place.

Heracles's nephew Iolaus helped him by burning the neck stumps when Heracles chopped off the heads to prevent new ones sprouting. The severed immortal head had to be buried under a huge rock, and Heracles finally cut open the Hydra's body and dipped his arrows in its venomous blood.

THE CENTAURS

Creatures with the upper body of a human and the lower body and legs of a horse

WHERE:
Living in caves in the mountains and forests of northern Greece, especially Mount Pelion

The Centaurs (Κένταυροι) were terrifying, flesh-eating, half-man, half-horse creatures. They hunted wild animals for food and often fought using rocks and the branches of trees. The Greeks called the great **battle that they fought against the Centaurs the "Centauromachy."**

This great battle happened when the Centaurs were invited to their half brother Pirithous's wedding. The Centaurs wreaked havoc at the party and tried to kidnap all of the women. One of them even tried to abduct the bride, and in the fight that followed, there were lots of casualties on both sides.

One of the Greek fighters was Caeneus, who had once been a woman but had been changed into an invulnerable man. But when the Centaurs attacked Caeneus, they couldn't find a way to kill him.

So instead, they piled a huge number of massive pine trees on top of him, and he gradually disappeared, still unconquered, into the earth. In the end, it was the Greeks who won the battle.

◇ Centaurs were half-man, half-horse. **Mostly they were horses with a human torso on top, and had four horsey legs**, but some of the early ones were a full human with a horse sticking out of the back, and had two human legs, and two equine ones. Female Centaurs were known as Centaurides.

◇ The Centaur Nessus tried to carry off Heracles's wife, Deianira, so Heracles shot him with an arrow poisoned with Hydra-venom. Nessus gave his blood-and-poison-soaked cloak to Deianira, telling her it was a love charm, but when she gave it to Heracles, it started to attack his flesh. **He tried to get the tunic off, but it stuck to his body and his flesh came away with it.**

◇ There were also some good Centaurs. **One of these was Chiron, who taught hunting, music, and medicine**. His student Achilles lived on a diet of lions and wild boars, bears, fawns, and deer, which gave him the strength and courage of the aggressive animals and the quickness of the others.

TYPHON

A monstrous serpentine Giant and the most deadly creature

WHERE:
Stretching from the east to the west and from the bottom of the sea to the Heavens

Typhon (Τυφῶν), also known as Typhaon and Typhoeus, was a nightmarish opponent of Zeus. He was a child of Gaia and was the ultimate monstrosity, a ghastly man-beast creature who was so massive that he towered over the mountains and his head scraped the stars. One of his hands could touch the west while the other touched the east.

Hissing, shouting, and spouting a great jet of fire from his mouth, Typhon attacked the Heavens with flaming rocks. All the gods except Zeus turned themselves into animals and ran away to Egypt, but Zeus fought Typhon with thunderbolts and a sickle. Typhon gripped Zeus in his snaky coils, wrenched the sickle from his hand, and cut the sinews of his hands and feet.

The monster then left the helpless god in a cave, hid the sinews in a bearskin, and told the she-dragon Delphyne to guard them.

Fortunately, Hermes and Goat-Pan stole the sinews and put them back into Zeus. Zeus showered Typhon with thunderbolts from a chariot of winged horses, and the Fates tricked Typhon into tasting the ephemeral fruits by saying that they would strengthen him. Typhon hurled mountains, which Zeus blasted back with thunderbolts, until Zeus finally heaved Mount Etna on top of him.

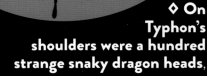

◇ **On Typhon's shoulders were a hundred strange snaky dragon heads**, all with black tongues darting out. His eyes flashed with fire from underneath his eyebrows, and fire blazed out from every head when he looked around. All kinds of astounding voices came from Typhon's weird heads.

◇ **The bottom part of Typhon was as gruesome as the top**: from the thighs down, he had huge coils of horrible hissing vipers instead of legs, his body was winged and covered in feathers, and wild disheveled hair streamed on the wind from his head and cheeks.

◇ When Typhon fought Zeus, a stream of blood gushed from Mount Haimos, "the Bloody Mountain" (*haima* means "blood" in Greek). **Mount Etna's volcanic eruptions were caused by the thunderbolts thrown in the tussle.** When Zeus finally imprisoned Typhon in Tartarus, he still caused devastating storms that came from the dark kingdom of the Underworld.

THE GRIFFIN

They guarded and made nests from the gold that could be found and mined there.

A lionlike beast with the wings and beak of an eagle

WHERE:
In a dreary mountain wilderness, in nests made of gold

The Griffin had lots of different names in Greek. They called it a Gryphon, Grypon, or a Gryps (γρύφων, γρύπων, or γρύψ). Griffins were four-legged animals that had enormously powerful lionlike claws. Their eyes flashed like fire, and they had a beak and a head like an eagle's, and wings that had exquisitely beautiful feathers. The goddess Athena sometimes wore a helmet with pictures of Griffins on it.

The creatures built their lairs in the mountains, where they guarded and made nests from the gold that could be found and mined there. The Arimaspians, a tribe of one-eyed people, would mount their fast horses and try to steal the gold from the Griffins. Meanwhile the Indians would go out and try to pick up any gold that fell out of the nests. The Griffins, who were afraid for their young, would fight back with all their might. Humans were so afraid of the strength of these beasts that they would only go in search of the gold at night so that they were less likely to be detected.

◇ **Griffins were famous for their feathers**. The creatures had powerful wings with black feathers running along their backs and red feathers covering their fronts. The wings themselves were white, and the necks of the creatures were adorned with beautifully patterned dark blue feathers.

◇ **Griffins were really ferocious** and would fight viciously with other beasts and easily overpower them. However, they were too scared of lions or elephants to ever face them.

◇ The gold seekers would travel in huge groups of up to 2,000 people, carrying weapons, spades, and sacks. They would wait for a dark and moonless night to make their move. **If they managed to get past the Griffins, they would take home their gold and use special skills to smelt it**.

THE GIANTS

Massive sons of Mother Earth

WHERE:
The Gigantomachy happened in northern Greece

Most of the Giants (Γίγαντες) were massive, mighty children of Gaia (Mother Earth). They had long hair on their heads and chins, and dragon scales covering their feet.

Gaia forced the Giants to take part in a huge battle against the gods, called the Gigantomachy. The Giants Alcyoneus, Porphyrion, Ephialtes, Eurytus, Clytius, Mimas, Enceladus, Polybotes, Hippolytus, Agrius, Thoas, and many others all attacked the sky with rocks and blazing oak trees.

An oracle predicted that the gods would only win the ferocious battle with the help of a mortal, so they recruited the mighty Heracles. Heracles began by shooting Alcyoneus with an arrow, but the Giant was immortal when he was in the land of his birth and recovered quickly. When Heracles discovered this, he dragged Alcyoneus out of his native land so he could kill him.

Zeus blasted the king of the Giants, Porphyrion, with a thunderbolt. Apollo and Heracles shot Ephialtes in each eye. Dionysus saw off Eurytus with his thyrsus (a type of spear). Hecate slew Clytius with her torches. Hephaestus slaughtered Mimas with missiles of red-hot metal. Athena eliminated Enceladus by hurling the island of Sicily onto him. Poseidon broke off part of the island of Cos and threw it onto Polybotes. Hermes wore the helmet of Hades, became invisible, and killed Hippolytus. The Fates battered Agrius and Thoas. Zeus and Heracles destroyed the rest of the Giants with thunderbolts and arrows.

◇ The Titan Atlas was another gigantic being who waged war against Zeus. **When he was defeated, he was forced to carry the Heavens on his shoulders and turn them so that the stars would rotate.** Eventually Perseus turned him into stone using the loathsome head of Medusa: Atlas the Giant became Atlas the mountain.

◇ Gaia's son Antaeus was a Giant who used to kill strangers by forcing them to wrestle with him. **He was invincible as long as he stayed in contact with his mother Earth**...so Heracles lifted him above his head and crushed him to death.

◇ **When the Giants Otus and Ephialtes were only nine years old, they were eighteen feet wide and 54 feet high.** They wanted to attack the gods, so they stacked mountains on top of each other to reach the sky. The gods were furious. Artemis, goddess of hunting, took revenge by tricking them. When the two Giants were out hunting, she changed herself into a deer, and in their haste to hit her, they shot each other.

CHIMAERA

◊ **Because she was a hybrid monster**, part-snake, part-goat, and part-lion, the Greeks gave her some special titles—Trikephalos, which means "three-headed," and Trisomatos, which means "three-bodied."

A monstrous fire-breathing creature

WHERE:
Lycia, in quite mountainous territory, then in Hades

Chimaera (Χίμαιρα) means "she-goat" in Greek. Some people said that the Chimaera was the child of the Giant Typhon and the "mother of all monsters" Echidna, who was half-woman, half-snake. The great Greek poet Homer described Chimaera as "a thing made by the immortals, not human, a lion at the front, a snake behind, and a goat in the middle, whose breath snorted out the terrible flame of blazing fire."

The Chimaera devastated all the country of Lycia (modern southwestern Turkey) and all its livestock, until the hero

Bellerophon mounted his winged horse Pegasus. With Pegasus's help, Bellerophon slew the Chimaera by shooting her from the air, well away from her heads and her fiery breath, and finished her off by using a spear tipped with a lump of lead, which melted in the monster's fiery breath and brought about her death.

◊ Some experts think that Christian pictures of **Saint George on his horse slaying the dragon** come directly from the story of Bellerophon riding on the back of Pegasus and slaying the Chimaera.

◊ **After Bellerophon killed her, the Chimaera "armed with flame" was stationed with many other monstrous beasts at the doors of the Underworld:** Centaurs, double-shaped Scyllas, the hundred-armed Briareus, the horrible hissing Hydra of Lerna, the Gorgons, the Harpies, and the gigantic ghost of three-bodied Geryon.

THE HUNDRED-HANDERS

Three Giants of incredible strength and ferocity

> "The Hundred-Handers held huge rocks in their mighty hands while the earth crashed loudly, the sky shivered and groaned, and Mount Olympus shook. "

WHERE:
In Tartarus

The three Hundred-Handers were known as the Hecatoncheires (Ἑκατόγχειρες). They were gigantic, powerful, violent creatures, and each of them had 100 arms and hands springing **from their shoulders, as well as 50 heads.**

They were the most terrible children of Ouranos (Sky) and Gaia (Mother Earth), who called them Cottus, Briareus, and Gyes. They were stubborn and arrogant, and Ouranos hated them from the moment they were born. In fact, he was so afraid of them that he immediately locked them away in the deep, dark dungeon of Tartarus.

However, Zeus unleashed them during the Titanomachy, his war against Gaia's other children, the Titans. It was an awesome battle: the two sides met with a great battle cry, and their shouting reached the stars of Heaven. The Hundred-Handers held huge rocks in their mighty hands while the earth crashed loudly, the sky shivered and groaned, and Mount Olympus shook. Zeus emerged victorious, and the Titans were imprisoned in Tartarus with Cottus, Briareus, and Gyes as their jailors.

◇ **The Hundred-Handers loved fighting and were at the front line in the Titanomachy war.** With their 300 hands, they launched 300 rocks, which crushed the Titans and buried them under the ground. The gigantic Hecatoncheires then bound the Titans in chains and imprisoned them far beneath the earth.

◇ **Tartarus was the deepest place in the world**—buried beneath the Underworld itself. It was so deep that a bronze anvil falling from the Earth would drop for nine days and nights, and only reach Tartarus on the tenth day.

◇ Cottus, Briareus, and Gyes each used their 100 hands to whip the clouds into a storm. Zeus allowed them to emerge from Tartarus every November at the rising of the Constellation of the Altar, **and they created bad weather all over Greece.**

MEDUSA

A winged monster, with living venomous snakes for hair

> " *Perseus flew to the land of the Gorgons, who were all fast asleep when he arrived...so Perseus grabbed his chance. He turned his gaze away and used a bronze shield to reflect their image.* "

◇ Medusa was once very beautiful, but she had the arrogance to compare her beauty to the goddess Athena's—never a good idea. **Because it was her hair that was particularly lovely, Athena turned it into snakes.**

◇ When Perseus returned with Medusa's head, he discovered that Polydectes had not been treating his mother very well. **So Perseus unleashed the Gorgon's head** and turned Polydectes into stone. He gave Medusa's head to Athena, and she placed it in the center of her snake-fringed aegis to terrify her enemies.

◇ **Perseus rescued Andromeda from being eaten by a sea monster.** He was going to marry her, but her ex-boyfriend turned up and tried to stop the wedding...So Perseus used Medusa's head to turn him and all his friends to stone.

WHERE:
In the west near the setting sun

There were three Gorgons: Medusa (Μέδουσα), whose name means Ruler, was the mortal one, and her two immortal sisters were called Stheno (Strength) and Euryale (Wide-leaping). They had heads that were covered in writhing snakes; large boarlike tusks; bronze hands; big, staring eyes; broad, round heads; wide mouths; lolling tongues; flared nostrils; short, coarse beards; and golden wings. And, most terrifyingly, they turned anyone who **looked at them into stone.**

The Greek hero Perseus boasted to his mother's admirer, King Polydectes, that he could slay Medusa and bring back her head. On his journey, some nymphs gave him a pair of winged sandals, a kind of messenger bag called the kibisis, and the cap of invisibility, while Hermes gave him a sickle made of a legendary stone called adamant.

Perseus flew to the land of the Gorgons, who were all fast asleep when he arrived...so Perseus grabbed his chance. He turned his gaze away, and used a bronze shield to reflect their image, and while the great goddess Athena guided his hand, he chopped off Medusa's head. Perseus stuffed her head into the kibisis and flew away. And though her sisters awoke and gave chase, it was no good: the cap of invisibility did its trick, and they couldn't find him.

THE MINOTAUR

A monster with the body of a man and the head and tail of a bull

WHERE:
In the Labyrinth at Knossos on Crete

When Minos wanted to become king of Crete, he asked the god of the sea, Poseidon, to send a bull from the sea, and promised to sacrifice it.

A magnificent white beast appeared and Minos became king, but he couldn't bear to slaughter the bull. Poseidon was furious, and to punish Minos, he made his wife, Pasiphae, fall in love with the bull.

The Minotaur (Μīνώταυρος) was Pasiphae and the bull's child.

"Minotaur" means "Bull of Minos," although his real name was Asterius ("the Starry One"). Horrified at this unnatural happening, Minos shut the Minotaur up in a Labyrinth—a complicated underground maze that was almost impossible to find your way out of.

Every year, the king of Athens, Aegeus, sent seven men and seven girls as food for the Minotaur. Aegeus's son Theseus was one of these young men. Minos's daughter Ariadne fell madly in love with Theseus, and to help him on his journey through the Labyrinth, she gave him a ball of thread to unwind as he went. He found the Minotaur, and they fought to the death. Theseus won and used the thread to find his way out again.

◇ The Minotaur had the body of a man and the head, shoulders, and tail of a bull. **The Labyrinth where he lived was full of confusing, winding passageways.** It was here that he attacked people with his horns until the day Theseus crushed him with his triple-knotted club.

◇ **The ship in which Theseus traveled had black sails.** Before he left, he promised his father that he would hoist scarlet sails if he returned alive. But Theseus forgot to do this. When his ship returned with black sails, Aegeus thought his son was dead. He threw himself from the cliffs in anguish, which is how the Aegean Sea

◇ **Ariadne only promised to help Theseus if he would take her back to Athens and marry her.** He agreed and they set sail together, but he then left her behind on the island of Dia. However, the god Dionysus arrived, fell in love with Ariadne, and married her.

◆ Cerberus was the loyal pet of Hades, the king of the Underworld. He lived close to the terrible River Styx, which the souls of the dead had to cross to reach their last resting place, and he was so massive that **he had a cave for his kennel.**

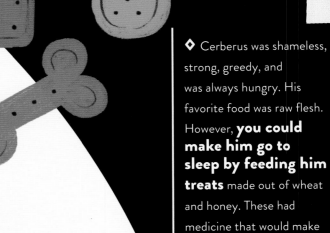

◆ Cerberus was shameless, strong, greedy, and was always hungry. His favorite food was raw flesh. However, **you could make him go to sleep by feeding him treats** made out of wheat and honey. These had medicine that would make him sleep hidden inside of them.

CERBERUS

A multi-headed dog that guards the gates of the Underworld

WHERE:

At the exit from the Underworld: he lets you in, but never out

Cerberus (Κέρβερος) was the multi-headed guard dog of the Underworld. His name means "Death-Demon of the Darkness," but often he was just called "the dog" or "the hound of Hades." He was a terrifying canine monstrosity and his triple-throated barks of frenzied rage would terrify even the ghosts of the dead. He would wag his tail and both his ears for anyone going down into the Underworld. But he would eat up anyone who tried to get out!

Very few have ever managed to get past this multi-headed beast and escape the Underworld. When the brilliant musician Orpheus went down into the Underworld to bring back his wife, Eurydice, he was able to get past Cerberus because the beauty of his music made the beast stand in awe and forget to bark.

Heracles had to fetch Cerberus from the Underworld as one of his Twelve Labors. The goddess Persephone helped him, but the mighty hero still had to wrestle with Cerberus, and one of the dog's snakes bit him. But Heracles still managed to drag him up a steep track while the beast struggled, and blinked, and screwed up his eyes against the blinding sunshine, which he had never seen before. Once the Labor had been completed, Heracles returned Cerberus to Hades.

◆ Cerberus had multiple dog heads (usually three, but some people say 50 or even 100). His tail was like a serpent, **and snake heads bristled all the way down his back.**

THE SIRENS

Dangerous creatures who lured nearby sailors with their enchanting music

WHERE:
An island called Anthemoessa

The Sirens (Σειρῆνες) were singing enchantresses who bewitched sailors with their melodies and lured them to their doom. They were monstrous sea nymphs, part-female humans, part-birds (from the thighs down).

They were incredible musicians—one played the lyre, one sang, and one played the pipes—and they used their amazingly beautiful music to lure sailors to their deaths on treacherous rocks. Jason and the Argonauts were able to sail past the Sirens thanks to the wondrous music of Orpheus, whose singing overcame the power of the Sirens' song.

When Odysseus had to sail past them, he really wanted to hear their famously beautiful song, so he told his crewmen to fill their ears with wax and made them tie him to the ship's mast and not let him go. The Sirens' song was so gorgeous that Odysseus kept begging to be released, but his men tied him even tighter. It had been prophesied that the Sirens would die when a ship managed to sail past them without stopping, and that out of pure anger and frustration they would throw themselves into the sea and be turned into rocks.

◇ Once upon a time, the Sirens had been handmaids of the goddess of harvest Demeter's daughter, Persephone. When the god of the Underworld, Hades abducted Persephone, **Demeter gave the Sirens the bodies of birds to help try to find her.** But in the end, they gave up looking and settled on the island of Anthemoessa.

◇ The Sirens had the fair faces of beautiful young girls, and the top halves of their bodies were human. The rest of them was birdlike, with wings, feathers, and claws. **Their voices were high and clear, and the sound of their singing sent everyone into raptures of delight.**

◇ **The goddess Hera persuaded the Sirens to have a singing competition with the Nine Muses.** Even though the Sirens' song was amazing and wonderful, the Muses still won, and they plucked out the Sirens' feathers to make crowns for themselves.

> " Jason and the Argonauts were able to sail past the Sirens thanks to the wondrous music of Orpheus. "

◇ **The Harpies were disgusting, feathered hybrid creatures.** They looked like ugly women with birds' wings, human arms, great talons for hands, and faces that were haggard with insatiable hunger. Their droppings smelled so horrible that no one could bear to go near them.

◇ When Aeneas was fleeing from Troy, the Harpies tore the Trojans' banquet to pieces and soiled everything with their foul touch. When the Trojans fought back, **Celaeno prophesied that for trying to kill the Harpies a terrible famine would force them to eat their own tables before they could build a new city.**

" They could move incredibly fast, and... would drop out of the clouds without any warning. "

THE HARPIES

Half-human, half-bird creatures

◇ **An oracle said that Zetes and Calais would kill the Harpies,** but that they themselves would die if they couldn't catch whoever they were chasing. Zetes and Calais pursued the Harpies to go to Strophades Islands (the Islands of Turning), but their lives were spared when it was agreed that they would stop attacking Phineus.

WHERE:
Salmydessus in northern Greece

The Harpies (ἄρπυιαι) were female spirits of sudden, sharp gusts of wind. They lived in the Land of Milk-Feeders and got their name because they would snatch things away (in Greek *harpazo* means "I snatch"). They could move incredibly fast, and like whirlwinds or lightning flashes, they would drop out of the clouds without any warning.

There were three Harpies—Aellopous, Celaeno, and Ocypete—and they tormented a blind old man named Phineus who was king of Salmydessus in Thrace. Phineus had the gift to see into the future and used this power to tell people about Zeus's plans. Zeus punished the old man by giving him lingering old age and taking away his sight. Whenever he was given any food, the Harpies flew down and snatched most of it up. Whatever was left stank so badly that no one could go near it.

The Argonauts helped Phineus by setting up a table as bait; when the shrieking Harpies swooped down, they were chased away by the winged sons of the North Wind, Zetes and Calais. Iris, the goddess of the rainbow, swore an oath that the Harpies would not torment Phineus ever again, and the creatures went to live in a cave on Crete.

THE PHOENIX

A long-lived bird that regenerates and is born again

WHERE:
Assyria, India, and Egypt

The Phoenix (φοῖνιξ) was a firebird that lived in Assyria and India. His feathers were gold and red, and he was similar in shape and size to an eagle.

The Phoenix lived for 500 years. When he knew that his life was nearing its end, he would fly to Egypt. Here he would gather sweet-smelling dry herbs, spices, and branches, and build a nest high on a lofty, swaying palm tree. Then he would settle down to wait for death, relaxing among the spicy perfumes.

His nest would become both his tomb and his cradle.

The Phoenix would sit in the nest and greet the sun, begging for its fires to renew his strength. The sun would then shine its heavenly life-giving light on the Phoenix, and the fragrant nest would burst into flames and burn the creature's old body. But then the ashes would start to show signs of new life and begin to move. Feathers would appear in the cinders, and a new little Phoenix would be born ready to live for another 500 years.

◇ The legs of the Phoenix were the same color as the most expensive purple clothes, and **it could fly faster than the wind** on wings of flowerlike blue that were dappled with rich gold.

◇ The Phoenix didn't eat normal bird food to satisfy its hunger, and it didn't quench its thirst with normal drink. **It fed on the oils of balsam and the tears of frankincense** and nourished itself with sunbeams and the spray from the sea.

> " the fragrant nest would burst into flames and burn the creature's old body. But then the ashes would start to show signs of new life and begin to move. "

◇ **The Phoenix's body gave out pure rays of sunshine and shone with gold.** A mysterious fire flashed from the creature's eyes, and a flaming halo surrounded its head. The bird had a crest that gleamed with the sun's own light and shattered the darkness with its soothing brilliance.

TALOS

A Giant made of bronze

WHERE:
On the shores of Crete

Talos (Τάλως) was a bronze Giant who Zeus gave to Europa to guard the island of Crete. Talos guarded the island by running around it three times every day, his bronze feet breaking massive rocks off the cliffs as he ran.

Zeus would then hurl these rocks at any sailors who tried to come near the island.

Jason and the Argonauts were sailing home to Greece after they had captured the Golden Fleece. They were frightened, tired, and thirsty. But Talos stopped them from coming onto the island. However, Medea the sorceress wouldn't stand for this and bewitched Talos's eyes with the evil in her own.

She flung the full force of her malevolence at him: summoned the Spirits of Death and called on the swift hounds of Hades, who feed on souls and haunt the lower air to pounce on living men. She sank to her knees and prayed three times in song, and three times with spoken words. The Argonauts watched in amazement as Talos's strong legs grew weak. He began to sway, all the power went out of him, and then he sank lifeless to the ground, falling down with a huge crash.

◆ Talos's body and limbs were made of bronze. He had just one blood-red vein, filled with ichor, the fluid which the gods have instead of blood. **There was only one place where he could be harmed, near his ankle, where his vein was only covered by very thin skin.**

◆ Talos was lifting up some immense rocks to hurl at the Argonauts to keep them from anchoring, but Medea's magic made him graze his ankle, which was his only weak point, against a jagged rock. **All the ichor in his body gushed out like molten lead. And then he collapsed in a lifeless heap.**

◆ Some said that Talos was a bronze statue who had been made by the god Hephaestus; others said he was a **descendant of the bronze race** that sprang from the ash trees, and that he had survived into the days of the demigods.

PEGASUS

A winged divine stallion

WHERE:
By springs, in the air, and on Mount Olympus

Pegasus (Πήγασος) was an immortal, winged horse. He was the offspring of Medusa and Poseidon. Medusa was pregnant with Chrysaor ("the Man with the Golden Sword") and Pegasus, when Perseus chopped her head off. Upon her death, the two children sprang from her neck.

Pegasus was tamed by the hero Bellerophon, and they made a fantastic team: with Pegasus's aid, Bellerophon slew the Chimaera, fought the warlike Solymi, engaged the Amazons in combat, and killed the bravest fighters of the Lycians.

Bellerophon had to do all of this fighting because a girl named Stheneboea had fallen in love with him.

However, Bellerophon rejected her, and in pure rage and spite, she accused him of attacking her.

Proetus, the king of Tiryns, believed the girl's accusations and sent Bellerophon to Stheneboea's father, Iobates, king of Lycia, with a sealed letter. The letter contained instructions that he was to kill Bellerophon. When Iobates read the letter, he ordered Bellerophon to fight the Chimaera, the Solymi, and the Amazons, thinking that he would never survive.

After their victories, Pegasus flew up to Olympus, where he became Zeus's thunderbolt bearer. In the end, Pegasus was put in the stars as a constellation. His appearance in the night sky marks the arrival of spring.

◇ The name Pegasus means either "sprung forth" because he sprang from the severed neck of the Gorgon Medusa, or **"of the spring,"** because Pegasus had links to various springs, especially Hippocrene (Horse Fountain) and the spring on Mount Helicon that inspired the Muses. This spring arose from a kick of his hoof.

◇ To tame the wondrous horse, Bellerophon slept on an altar where he dreamed that Athena gave him a golden bridle and ordered him to sacrifice a white bull to Poseidon, Tamer of Horses. **In the morning, he found the golden bridle beside him, sacrificed the bull, and Pegasus willingly accepted him.**

◇ **Bellerophon took vengeance on Stheneboea** by giving her a ride on Pegasus and pushing her off over the sea.

❝ His appearance in the night sky marks the arrival of spring. ❞

To my muses: lovely-haired Lal, and keen-scenting Hero. —S.K.

To Joe and Jazz. —V.T.

Brimming with creative inspiration, how-to projects, and useful information to enrich your everyday life, Quarto Knows is a favorite destination for those pursuing their interests and passions. Visit our site and dig deeper with our books into your area of interest: Quarto Creates, Quarto Cooks, Quarto Homes, Quarto Lives, Quarto Drives, Quarto Explores, Quarto Gifts, or Quarto Kids.

Mythologica © 2019 Quarto Publishing plc.
Text © 2019 Steve Kershaw.
Illustrations © 2019 Victoria Topping.

First Published in 2016 by Wide Eyed Editions, an imprint of The Quarto Group.
400 First Avenue North, Suite 400, Minneapolis, MN 55401, USA.
T (612) 344-8100 F (612) 344-8692 **www.QuartoKnows.com**

The right of Victoria Topping to be identified as the illustrator and Steve Kershaw to be identified as the author of this work has been asserted by them in accordance with the Copyright, Designs and Patents Act, 1988 (United Kingdom).

A catalog record for this book is available from the British Library.

ISBN 978-1-78603-193-8

The illustrations were collaged and drawn digitally
Set in Brandon Grotesque, Cherry Swash, and Sagarana

Published by Jenny Broom and Rachel Williams
Designed by Nicola Price
Edited by Claire Grace
Production by Nicolas Zeifman

Manufactured in Guangdong, China PP052019

9 8 7 6 5 4 3 2 1